DESCENT II™

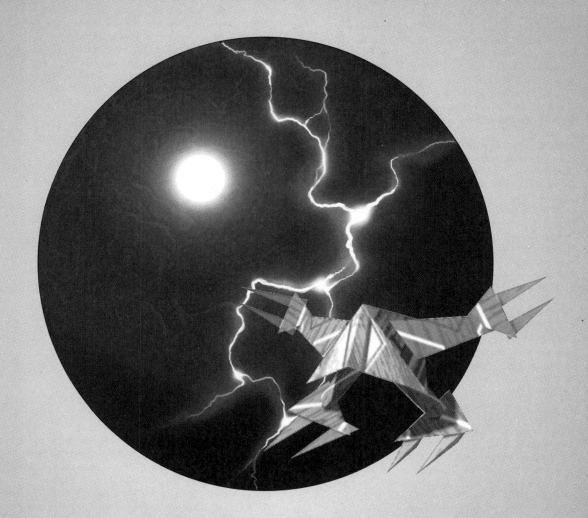

THE OFFICIAL
STRATEGY GUIDE

NOW AVAILABLE FROM PRIMA

How to Order:

DESCENT II

THE OFFICIAL STRATEGY GUIDE

Raphael Hernandez

Matthew J. Norton

PRIMA PUBLISHING

Project Editor: Dallas Middaugh

ISBN: 0-7615-0291-2
Library of Congress Catalog Card Number: 95-70656
Printed in the United States of America
96 97 98 BB 10 9 8 7 6 5 4 3 2 1

CONTENTS

FOREWORD

Descent and *Descent II* were developed by Parallax Software, founded in June, 1993 by Matt Toschlog and Mike Kulas. Both of them had substantial experience in flight simulators and in arcades during the 1980s. Their desire with *Descent* was to bring together the action from a 1980s arcade game with a flight simulator in a very rich environment.

The original proposal for what became *Descent* was written in 1992 and was developed into a script in the spring of 1993. Work began in June, 1993 and the full version of *Descent* I shipped in March, 1995. *Descent II* began as a minor enhancement to *Descent*, but it grew to become a major sequel, with numerous significant enhancements. It shipped in March, 1996.

The *Descent II* development team consists of Kulas, Toschlog, Adam Pletcher, Jasen Whiteside, Mark Dinse, Doug Brooks, Jason Leighton, Samir Sinha, Mark Allender, Jeremy Sandmel, Rob Huebner, and Che-Yuan Wang. With the exception of Kulas and Toschlog, *Descent* and *Descent II* represent the first game industry experience for the team. We believe the desire to create a game which we found fun to play, coupled with a willingness to polish it for months has yielded something original. We hope you'll agree.

— The *Descent* Team

ACKNOWLEDGMENTS

Matthew J. Norton would like to dedicate this book to Monica Norton with thanks and appreciation for all those years.

Raphael Hernandez would like to dedicate this book to his parents, with special thanks, Aida Hernandez and Raphael Hernandez, Sr.

Both of us would like to thank a few special people without whom this book would have been much more difficult, if not impossible;

Marti "Mom" Cadenasso, for her faith and unwavering support
Jason "The Gunn" Suinn, for his tenacious mapping skills
Chris "Stickman Theatre" Avellone, for last minute penmanship
Late Night (5 hour-old) Gritty Black Coffee

All of our friends and coworkers (same thing) for putting up with us for the last couple of months, and, of course,

All the Great People at both Interplay and Parallax without whom this game would not be the Great Fun that it is (and without whom this book would not have been possible).

INTRODUCTION
HOW TO USE THIS BOOK

When *Descent* released in 1995 it was an international success. Its notoriety grew quickly, moving from popular to best-selling to phenomenon in just a few short months. Even before the full version appeared in stores, it was the rage of the Internet. People played the demo, and they wanted more, so they bought the game. Then they played the game from beginning to end, and they wanted more—but they had to wait. Now the wait is over. *Descent II* is here. And you, the die-hard fan, have what you need to get you safely through every mine, every chasm, every lava pit, every secret level—*Descent II: The Official Strategy Guide*.

This book is broken up into four parts. The first part, Intelligence Reports, gives you the tips and strategies you need to get through these mines intact. Here you will learn how to best maneuver your ship, the threat levels of your robotic enemies, the effects of the various weapons and powerups available to you, and what to expect from the dastardly Mine Bosses.

The second part, Mission Maps, provides you with maps that will let you know exactly what robot is waiting for you around the corner, and where all those special goodies are hidden. Detailed walkthroughs describe how to get from the beginning to the blue key, to the yellow key, to the red key, to the reactor, and then to the all-important exit.

The third part, Secret Levels, gives you everything you need to locate and navigate the six hidden areas in *Descent II*.

Finally, the fourth part, Multiplayer *Descent II*, gives you tips and hints for beating your fellow pilots into the ground.

We've given you all the help we can. From here on out you're on your own. Learn fast and you may live to see the dawn.

PART 1

INTELLIGENCE REPORTS

Preliminary Data

Status: Confidential

Transmission: 574.873.11 Alpha

To: Material Defender *in situ*

From: Dravis, Production-Cost-Control-Department, PTMC, Mines Division

Material Defender, in order to maximize your chances of success on this containment mission it is necessary for you to know certain facts.

Note: Any information that you may receive from PTMC regarding Mine Operations will be regarded as confidential. Any unauthorized disclosure of this information will be regarded as a breach of operational security and a) will serve as grounds for the termination of your contract, b) will disallow any access to further PTMC facilities (including repair and recovery ships), and c) due to the vital nature of PTMC's mining interests you will be treated as a trespasser if found near any PTMC facilities. Use of terminal force will be authorized in your apprehension and detainment—pending further legal action.

You will receive information on your ship and the most effective flight tactics to use while in the mines. You will also receive information regarding your ship's weaponry and the most effective way to use that weaponry. Each weapon system that you may have access to within the mines will be explained in detail and the most efficient use of each weapon will be discussed. You will also be shown other objects and features. Some of these are features of the mines themselves, while others are objects that you can pick up to increase the combat effectiveness of your ship.

Finally, you will receive the very latest intelligence reports on the robots you will be encountering. This information is based on passive sensors that are still active within parts of the mines and also on active reconnaissance probes.

You must use every bit of your skill and all the information that we will be providing if you are to fulfill all operational goals, Material Defender. Learn well. Both the mission and your life depend upon it.

Flight Operations

Status: Confidential

Transmission: 395.005.34 Delta

To: Material Defender *in situ*

From: Capt. Roy Eindecker, Flight Operations, PTMC, Security Division

I don't know who they got to fill the role of Material Defender this time, but I'm sure glad it's not me. All that reward money sounds good. And I wouldn't mind a peak at the executive washroom either. But that money isn't going to do you any good if your component atoms get spread all over another star-system. Even worse, they might have to look for someone inside the company to do the job.

Let's just make sure you don't fail, Material Defender. You could say that we both have a vested interest in that.

First, let's take a look at the ship you're using.

Ship Systems

1. **Avionics Bay:** Normally houses both active and passive radar, as well as Forward Looking Infa-Red camera bays. Now replaced by Experimental Warp-Core drive-unit. This area also contains room for an Energy to Shield conversion unit—currently uninstalled.

2. **Upper Wing with Hardpoints:** Has two hardpoints for mounting weapons. Currently equipped with two aerodynamic missile pods per wing for a total capacity of four missile storage pods.

1 Avionics Bay

2 Upper Wing with Hardpoints

3 Missile Storage Pods

4 Primary Thrusters

5 Lower Wing Primary Laser Armament

6 Armored Cockpit

3. **Missile Storage Pods:** Handle a variety of Missiles. Automatic stowage and cycling allow the pilot to fire any of the Missiles carried in any order. Aerodynamic nose housing slides back to allow missiles to fire.

4. **Primary Thrusters:** Two High-capacity V-goe engines. Hydraulic actuated Flex-ducting allows the full force of the thrusters to be redirected to allow the Pyro-GX to move backwards as fast as it can move forwards. These engines are suitable for use with a Winged-Mercury afterburner—currently uninstalled.

5. **Lower Wing, Primary Laser Armament:** Four wing mounted hardpoints allow the Pyro-GX to carry up to four laser cannons. Two are currently installed and active although the positions are shown as prepared for field-capable upgrade to a quad mounted laser cannon system. Note: Quad mounted lasers require the acquisition of the quad laser cooling, power, and focusing package—currently uninstalled.

6. **Armored Cockpit:** A Glassteel armored canopy protects a Titanium armored tub that encloses the pilot. The normal ejection package has been removed to allow for extended endurance during this mission.

The Pyro-GX is a good ship for her age, Material Defender. Reliable, nimble, quick. And even more important to you, she's built tough. Not a pretty ship, but built to survive. Be a shame to lose a museum piece like that one. Let's try to bring her back in one piece.

Survival Techniques

Here are the tips that will make the difference between success and failure out there.

It's all pretty simple, really. Just hit the enemy and keep hitting them until there aren't any more of them to blast. Of course, you have to avoid getting hit yourself while you're doing that. That's the tough part.

PART 1   Intelligence Reports

We've developed a simple acronym to help you remember what's important. It all comes down to F.A.T.E. really.

Fire control

Avoid enemy shots

Terrain advantage

Even the odds

Fire Control

Fire control is all-important. You will have limited resources in the mines, Material Defender. You must use the proper weapon for each circumstance. You must aim your shots. Spraying and praying will get you the short trip out of the mines. The one exception is when you have easy access to a nearby energy center. If you can easily replenish your energy reserves then it can be advantageous to fire more liberally than you would otherwise. Generally speaking though, careful aim and conserving ammunition and power will be your best bet for success.

Avoid Enemy Shots

Avoiding enemy fire is the only way to survive this mission. If you trade ordnance with the enemy shot-for-shot you will not exit the mines. The robots can make any number of mistakes; you don't get so many chances. It is always better to dodge enemy fire than it is to sit still in order to make a better shot yourself. The best way to avoid enemy fire is to slide sideways. The slide is the life. To slide you may either use your hat (if your joystick has one) or press Alt as you move. This will allow you to slide as you move. Robots have difficulty tracking this sliding movement.

As you slide you should keep your own guns trained upon your target. With practice you should be able to slide all the way around your target as you turn. This way you can continue to fire at your target at the same time that you are avoiding their return fire. If you turned your ship away from the enemy instead of sliding then you would not be able to fire at them until you had re-aimed your ship at them.

Although sliding up and down is equally effective as sliding to the left and right, you will suffer less disorientation if you only slide horizontally (at least at first).

Avoiding direct fire weapons is simply a case of being where they're not. Do not stay in any one place when you are being fired upon. Movement equals survival. In some rooms it may be difficult to determine where enemy fire is coming from. You must locate the firing robot if you are to be able to dodge that foe's shots. Once you locate all robots firing at you, you may have to make a rough estimate of relative danger. Dodge the shots that are going to hurt the most if you can only dodge some of the shots directed at your ship. If you are being fired upon by non-guided missiles, stay away from walls. Even if you are not hit by a missile, if it hits the wall next to you your ship could still be damaged by splash-fire.

Dodging homing weapons takes a little bit more skill. The best way to do this is to duck around a sharp corner or through a door if you can. Most missiles cannot turn quickly enough to hit you if you make a fast turn around a corner. If you cannot get behind cover quickly enough, you must attempt to dodge the homing shots in the open. The best way to do this is to wait until the shots are close and then suddenly and sharply slide out of the missile's path.

Terrain Advantage

Use terrain to your advantage. There are many places to hide and to shield your ship from enemy fire within the mines. You must use this to your benefit; the robots certainly will use it to theirs. Do not fly into the middle of a room to fight a robot opponent if you can hit him from a location that would allow you to duck and return fire.

Although, it's energy inefficient and I would not usually recommend it, sometimes you can expose only one wing of your ship to fire your wing-mounted lasers at a foe while the rest of your ship remains behind cover.

There is one more thing that will help you in the mines: Try to keep the lights above you and the floor tiles below your ship. The robots don't care which way is up or down and neither will you, eventually. But until you get used to the mines it will be easier for you to figure out where you are on the maps and to maintain you balance if you keep track of *up* and *down*. Use the auto-leveling feature to help you with this. In order to use this hit F2 and then select 'Toggles.' Auto leveling is one of the toggle selections.

Even the Odds

The robots outnumber you. If you allow them the opportunity, they will swarm your ship and you will be blown to bits. You must take it upon yourself to even the odds. Do not allow yourself to be drawn into a room full of robots if there is any possible way to avoid it. Make the robots come to you.

Most of the robots are very aggressive. This can be used to your advantage. Show enough of yourself to excite a robot's attack programming, then back away. Often you can draw individual robots out of a room full of them. Individual robots are much easier to deal with than groups of them. Anytime you can use tactics like this to snipe at lone robots (or even small groups), you should do so.

Simple patience is an extremely effective technique for eliminating robots. In most cases, taking your time and backing through previously cleared areas of the mines while you fight solitary pursuers is much better than flying into a room full of robots with all guns blazing.

Remember, Material Defender, heroism is surviving, not going out with the biggest explosion. If you have to, don't be too stupid to 'bug-out' of a bad situation and to try again after replenishing your power, your nerve, or both. If you have found an afterburner use it to make good your escape. Live to fight another day. You don't win this war by dying for good old PTMC—you win by making those damn bots die for whatever alien masters they serve now.

Good luck and good hunting, Material Defender.

Captain Eindecker out.

Weapon Descriptions

Status: Confidential

Transmission: 438.267.12 Alpha

To: Material Defender *in situ*

From: J. Smith, Chief Research Engineer, PTMC, Mines Division

Re: Cost Effective Weapons Use

CC: Dravis

Material Defender, I have been instructed by the Production-Cost-Control-Department to brief you on the most cost effective use of any experimental-mining-tools that you may find in the mines.

I want to make clear to you that PTMC does not now, nor have we ever, developed weapons. It is true that we have been experimenting with technologies *similar* to those used by the military for weaponry. However, Mr. Dravis has instructed me to reassure you that the items you find within the mines are for mining purposes only.

For ease of pilot identification we will refer to the various experimental-mining-tools as "weapons"—for the duration of this memo only.

It is fortunate for you, Material Defender, that tools developed for boring through the hardest rock also slice through military-grade titanium-composite armor with ease. It is also fortunate for you that field tests of these advanced weapons were relatively common throughout our outer-rim facilities. We have configured your Pyro-GX ship with a flexible auto-install system that should allow you to make use of any weapon that you find within the mines; this system can be engaged by simply flying over the weapon. Changing between weapons, once you find them, is done simply by hitting one of the number keys on your computer's keyboard.

Each of the number keys on your keyboard (except for 1 which always selects your best laser) toggles between two weapons. Hitting each number key once will bring up the first weapon attached to that key. Hitting the same number again will toggle your weapon selection to the other weapon attached to that key (provided you have equipped your ship with both weapons). Example: pressing ③ once will arm select the spreadfire cannon, pressing ③ a second time will change your weapon to the helix cannon.

Also, the default settings for weapons attached to your primary fire button (or both Left and Right Ctrl keys) are numbered 1-5, weapons attached to your secondary fire button (or Spacebar) are numbered 6-10.

Unfortunately for you, the alien robots also seem to have been able to equip themselves with the same advanced weaponry and show no reluctance in using it against intruders. In fact, research probes report that the aliens seem to have improved upon some of our designs.

Each of the weapons to be found in the mines has distinct strengths and weaknesses. In order to succeed with your mission, Material Defender, it is vital that you use the best weapon for each tactical situation.

First we will discuss direct fire weapons, then missiles and mines.

Pay close attention, Material Defender, these tips could save a life; namely, yours.

Direct Fire Weapons

These weapons are your primary armed response to tactical threats. They tend to have a higher rate of fire and your ship can carry far more shots of these than it can missiles and mines, since most of these weapons use energy directly from your fusion storage batteries.

If you have already equipped your ship with a weapon and then you fly over a duplicate of the weapon your ship will harvest energy or ammunition from the unit the weapon. With lasers this will only happen once you have already upgraded to a level four Laser.

One thing to keep in mind, Material Defender: More shots does not mean *unlimited* shots. If you fight your way through the mines with your finger perpetually on the fire button, you will quickly find yourself in a room full of hostile alien robots, out of energy, out of time, and out of luck.

Quick controlled bursts, and selecting the right weapon for the job, will help you to preserve your energy and your life.

Lasers

These are your standard armament. We were able to allow your ship to retain two modified AG 435 Argon-Cyanide Industrial Lasers despite installing your new Hyperdrive unit because the Lasers are field proven and reliable.

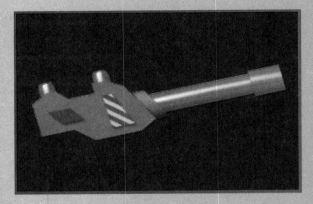

PTMC has been working on more efficient lasers that produce an increase in the amount of damage done without using any more energy. Since the technologies used are basically just improvements in the original design, your ship is designed to cannibalize any necessary parts to upgrade your existing lasers to the next level of power any time you pick up another laser within the mines. You may field-upgrade your laser, one step at a time, up to a level four laser just by flying over any laser you see in the mines.

Your laser is your friend. The laser is probably the best all around weapon you will find. Its low energy cost per shot coupled with high damage output (especially with an upgraded laser) make this your best bet for flying into unknown areas. The relatively high rate of fire means that at most ranges only the most agile robots will be able to dodge your shots.

Quad Lasers

This is a new coupling, focusing, and linking system for your lasers. The increase in cooling and focusing efficiency possible through this new weapons mount means that your ship now has twice as many lasers. With the quad laser in your ship four, laser shots rip out for each pull of the trigger rather than just two. Not only do your lasers do more damage but the area that your shots cover is somewhat wider as well.

Since the quad laser mounts two of your Lasers farther out on the wings, you can poke just a wing around a corner to shoot at opponents that you are not exposed enough to see from your ship's cockpit. This takes practice and plenty of spare energy but is extremely useful in some situations. This works with other weapons as well, but is most effective with the quad lasers.

Superlasers

This unusual looking laser is an experimental design that utilizes twice the number of coolant and focusing materials. Picking this up will dramatically increase your laser's power.

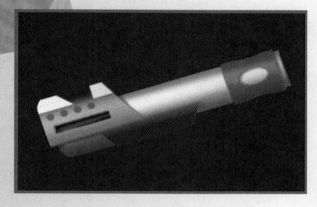

The only way to upgrade your lasers to level five and level six is by picking up a superlaser. Level six lasers are the strongest in the game, and when coupled with the quad laser mount this is arguably the best weapon to burn robots in the mines. The superlaser's low energy cost, high damage, and good rate of fire make this weapon worth looking for.

Vulcan Cannon

The vulcan cannon is an extremely fast-firing projectile weapon. Unlike most of your ship's weapons the vulcan cannon uses Armor-Piercing Depleted-Uranium (APDU) bullets rather than drawing energy from your fusion batteries. Rotating cryogenically-cooled barrels keep the gun from overheating. A single bullet does not do much damage but the gun's high rate of fire (the highest you will find in the mines) sends a torrent of white-hot death streaming toward your target.

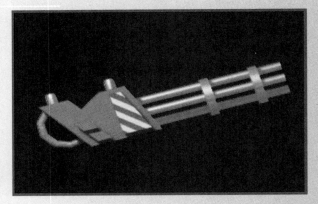

Some pilots like to save their vulcan cannon and Gauss Gun for times when they are running low on energy. Since both of these weapons fire bullets they are still able to be fired even when you have depleted your ship's fusion batteries. Often, this gives the pilot enough "fight-time" to get to an energy center to refuel. Of course, if you run out of both energy and bullets . . .

The shells from a vulcan cannon are fast enough to cross even the largest rooms instantaneously. The speed of the vulcan's shells is also too fast for robots to dodge. This makes the vulcan cannon the ultimate long-range sniper weapon. However, that same pinpoint precision makes the vulcan a poor choice for close-combat since it takes longer to aim with this weapon. The vulcan cannon must be used judiciously as it chews through shells at an alarming rate. Frequent users should keep a ready eye on the amount of ammunition remaining. The last thing a pilot needs is to run out of ammunition at a crucial moment.

Gauss Gun

The gauss gun is a refinement of the vulcan cannon. Using strong electromagnets, the gauss gun is able to propel shells forward at an incredible speed. The gauss gun uses the same APDU shells used by the vulcan cannon. However, since the gauss gun uses several powerful electromagnets rather than a chambered explosion to propel its shells, it can use several barrels at once without overheating the weapon. The tight pattern of high velocity shells expelled by the gauss gun with each shot make it the equivalent of the world's largest assault shotgun. Also, when the gun's shot hits an enemy robot, the impact from the blast causes both damage and a moment of disorientation as the target is knocked back several meters by the force of the blow. This knock-back effect can often give a pilot some much needed breathing room.

The gauss is the weapon of choice in long range fire-fights since, even across large rooms, shots fired by the gauss are so fast that dodging them is impossible. For closer range combats the tight pattern of shots fired by the gun means that a pilot must aim carefully, which is not always easy to do in a swirling dogfight. The knock-back effect from a good hit by the gauss may be useful at close range in some situations. Forcing claw-equipped

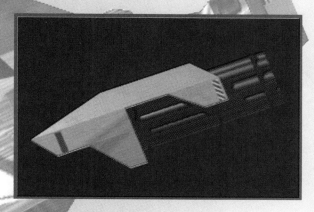

robots away from your ship is a lot easier when you can blast them off you.

The gauss gun does use up ammunition at a very high rate, but it does much more damage for the same number of shells expended than the vulcan cannon. Given a choice, the better pilot will always use a gauss gun rather than the vulcan cannon.

The Ammo Rack

This is not a weapon itself but it is an essential piece of equipment for any pilot that "goes to guns" frequently. We here at Mines R&D developed an experimental attachment that allows your Pyro-GX to carry twice the normal load-out of APDU shells. This experimental device does not burden your ship in any way—and, contrary to popular rumors, it does not make your ship any more prone to spontaneous explosions.

Our ammo rack allows you to carry 20,000 shells rather than the normal capacity of 10,000. Of course, you do still have to find the extra 10,000 shells yourself. However, Material Defender, you should not consider acquisition of the ammo rack an excuse to "hose

down" the entire mine with APDU shells. Even with the rack installed you will find that you can still run out of shells in a big hurry if you fire carelessly.

The ammo rack is extremely useful for carrying additional shells for your cannons. The ammo rack does give your ship additional storage space for missiles as well. This secondary capability of the ammo rack is just another thoughtful bonus from PTMC R&D.

Spreadfire Cannon

The spreadfire cannon was one of our first experiments with variable-focus energy-projection-optics. Using an alternating-focus system we designed the spreadfire for boring out wide ore-transport-tunnels through softer rock. The spreadfire shoots three energy particles in alternating vertical and then horizontal rows. Each energy particle does not do much damage since the spreadfire cannon was designed to spread out the damage over a wide area.

For destroying robots this weapon should be implemented in two ways. The deadliest use is to get close enough to your target so that all three energy particles from each shot hit the same target. The cumulative effect of so many shots is deadly. The next best use is for firing into large groups of opponents. A good pilot should use a "shoot and dodge" technique. Shoot the spreadfire cannon while flying evasively (the best way to fly when confronted by multiple foes). When dodging enemy fire

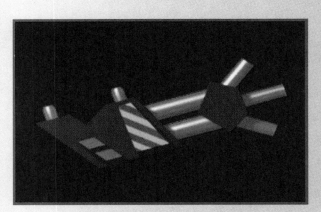

you may not be able to take careful aim for each shot, but if you are using the spreadfire cannon some of your shots should still strike home. Both of these techniques work best at short range. At medium or longer ranges the spreadfire's shot dispersion is too wide to target enemies effectively.

This weapon does deplete energy reserves twice as fast a Lasers so it should be used only when circumstances warrant. Because of the dispersion of their shots, both the spreadfire cannon and the helix cannon are great for clearing mines out of the path of your ship.

Helix Cannon

The helix cannon is an experimental advance over the spreadfire cannon. The shot-focus chambers have been designed to rotate through 360° rather than just alternating between vertical and horizontal. Advanced coolant technology has been used to allow the helix cannon to fire five shots with each pull of the trigger. The increased number of shots and the full arc of fire allows the helix cannon to scour corridors and small rooms clean of robot infestations.

If you can find any of the helix cannon prototypes within the mines you should use them in roughly the same situations that you would use the spreadfire cannon. One cautionary note: The helix cannon disperses its shots wider than the spreadfire cannon, so if you need to concentrate its firepower on a solitary target you will need to fire at closer range than you would with the spreadfire cannon.

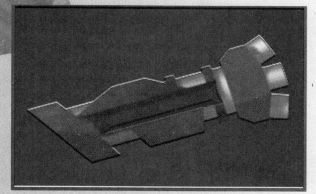

Plasma Cannon

The plasma cannon fires bursts of supercharged plasma at an extremely high rate of fire. We developed the plasma cannon initially for conduit tunneling but found it to be very useful against other corporation's spy probes. The high rate of fire allows a pilot to see where the shots are striking and to correct his aim based on the impact area. A good pilot can trace, or

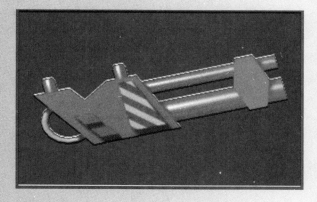

"walk," the stream of supercharged plasma shots onto the selected target and keep the shots "on target" until the target is eliminated. This ability allows a good pilot to be extremely accurate. Even though each shot of the plasma cannon does only a small amount of damage, the weapon blasts out a lot of shots very quickly.

Because of the plasma cannon's high rate of fire and the ability to walk shots onto a target this weapon is good at all ranges. At long range you can walk plasma onto a target just like moving a garden hose. Up close you can "spray and pray" since you will almost certainly get some shots in target area no matter how hard you're dodging enemy fire.

As you may have come to expect, Material Defender, all of this is not without cost. Each shot takes its toll on your ship's fusion batteries and you can very rapidly end up with nothing but empty fuel cells if you are not careful.

Phoenix Cannon

The phoenix cannon appears to be a hybrid-weapon developed by the aliens. Our reconnaissance drones show that the cannon uses power supplies that appear to be compatible with those in your ship, and you should be able to use the phoenix cannon if you can find one. Our probes show that the phoenix cannon shoots high temperature plasma balls that are held together with some kind of repulsor-field technology. The phoenix cannon's shots are actually able to bounce up to three times before exploding. If the shots hit a ship, robot, light, or switch before their third bounce they will explode. We believe that the same field that holds the shot together enough to bounce also dampens the damage potential of the weapon. However, all observations show an extremely high rate of fire for the weapon, which may help to mitigate the low damage per shot.

If you are able to capture one of these weapons extreme caution must be exercised in its use, Material Defender. Bouncing shots will cause damage to your own ship. Do not fire at walls directly in front of your ship with this weapon. Also be aware of possible reflecting shots coming from other directions. Do not experiment with this weapon if you are low on shields.

The same deflection qualities that make the phoenix cannon dangerous to use also make it a very useful tool if used prudently. You can virtually play pool with the deflecting shots, using field-bound plasma balls to sink alien robots into a corner pocket from which there is no return. The phoenix cannon can be used to bounce shots around corners and down hallways from angles which do not allow the enemy to return fire.

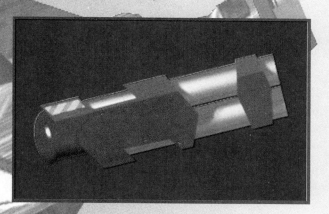

The need to generate a containing field for each shot along with the high rate of fire would lead us to believe that the energy requirements will be high for this weapon. Do not neglect your power gauge when you are using this weapon, Material Defender. Remember: Energy equals life down in the mines.

Internal PTMC memo

Employees are henceforth instructed not to speculate upon the requirements for entry authority into the executive lavatory facilities. Entry is only allowed to staff grades 15 (Ultraviolet) or higher, and their chosen guests.

—Dravis

By the way, we here at Mines division R&D would be very pleased with you if you could return to us with one of these weapons intact. Mr. Dravis himself has intimated that the keys to the executive washroom would fall into the hands of the first lucky pilot to return a phoenix cannon to PTMC for study.

Fusion Cannon

The fusion cannon is a more compact version of our heavy core drill. Usually the fusion cannon can only be mounted on heavy tracked vehicles like our planetary class boring vehicle. We reduced the size of the fusion cannon enough to fit into a main battle tank as well. We

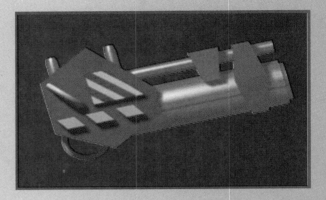

have managed to reduce the size even further (small enough to fit into your ship) but unfortunately the power drain could not be reduced. The only way we can get enough power to fuel the fusion cannon is to vent energy directly from your ship's own fusion reactor. The firing of this incredibly destructive device will have a noticeable effect upon your ship. The venting of energy from your ship's reactor will cause your ship to kick backwards several meters when you fire this weapon—do not be alarmed, your ship's recoil dampeners have just been overloaded by the fusion cannon's blast. They will come back online almost immediately. Many pilots also experience a pink glow throughout the cockpit—again, do not be alarmed, this is merely trace levels of radiation escaping harm- lessly through your ship's ventilation system.

One safety tip: Fire the fusion cannon as soon as it is charged or the vents from your ship's reactor will overheat and your ship will take dam- age. As long as you hold the fusion cannon charged (with the trigger down) your ship will continue to take damage. Timing is all important with this weapon, Material Defender.

The awesome destructive power of the fusion cannon is often worth the energy drain of firing it. A single blast will destroy most small to medium sized robots and severely damage even the most heavily armored foes. Groups of smaller robots can be destroyed by a single well-placed shot as well.

Venting your ship's reactor to fuel this weapon cannot be done too many times if you wish to have enough power remaining to fire other weapons. The need to charge the weapon each time before firing means a very slow rate of fire as well. Foes can often dodge out of your line of fire while the weapon is charging up and you should not hold your fire for long or your ship will take damage. However, despite all of the contraindications for the fusion cannon's use, in the right situations the fusion cannon is a Material Defender's best friend. The trick is knowing the right situations, such as when confronted by large, slow, tough or 'Boss' robots at close to medium range and when fighting large groups of robots at close to medium range. Long range shots and shots against fast moving or agile targets are not recommended as the target may easily avoid the shot, and the act of holding fire while aiming these shots may damage your ship.

Omega Cannon

The omega cannon is an experimental device that makes use of homing technology with a direct arc-fire weapon. The plasma arc that the omega cannon shoots will attempt to hit a target within a narrow cone of your aim-point. The plasma-arc will twist about like a bolt of lightning until it contacts a target, then it will attempt to stay locked-on to the target until the target is destroyed.

Naturally, as an experimental weapon this technology is less than perfect. The lock-on ability of the weapon is extremely limited. If you or the target move too much, then the weapon will lose target acquisition and must be targeted again. The weapon requires its capacitors be recharged for a time equal to the amount of time you have fired it. Use this weapon in controlled bursts for best effect. Also, the incredible destructive power of the omega cannon has a limited range; it is the only direct fire weapon that has a limited range, and you should only use this against targets at close to medium

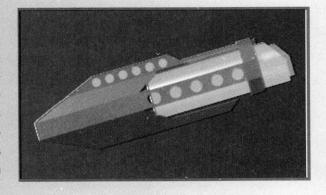

ranges. This cannon uses its arcing plasma to bore holes right through targets. The damage done by this weapon (for each second on-target) is higher than any other direct-fire weapon you will have access to in the mines.

One warning, Material Defender: The backblast from close range shots will almost certainly destroy your own ship. Fire this weapon with discretion. Use it as a scalpel, not a machete, and you will be well pleased with its effects.

Flares

These projectiles can be launched from your ship in virtually unlimited numbers. It does take some energy to fire them and they do minimal damage. They will stick to almost any hard surface and will provide illumination for a few seconds.

Pilot Flight Memo 943.35.245 Tango

Re: 'Flaring'

It has come to the attention of the Production-Cost-Control-Department that some pilots have been destroying enemy robots and even rival Corporation's reconnaissance probes using only Flares. This is apparently done to show disdain for what the pilots believe to be a weaker foe. However, even a weak foe can turn around and substantially damage PTMC property (i.e. your ship). Surviving pilots who continue to disdain the use of proper weapons will be remanded to service on Orbital Ore Barges from which they can exercise their 'Flare' 36 times a day as they illuminate the docking bays of automated Ore Conveyors on the dark side of Neptune.

—Dravis

They are somewhat useful for exploring darkened rooms. They are even more useful for highlighting cloaked (invisible) robots. If you suspect alien robots to be cloaked, flares should help you to see enough of their outlines to target them. However, for brief light use your lasers. They light up an area almost as well as flares do and cost less energy. If you are shooting into a darkened room there is always the chance that you will actually damage an enemy robot with the Laser whereas the Flare would only antagonize your foe.

Missiles and Mines

These weapons have the potential to inflict more damage per shot to your foes than direct fire weapons. However, they are slower firing and you will usually have no more than a few of any one type of missile or mine available at any one time. When used properly, mines and missiles will make the difference between getting out of a mine intact or as a cloud of radioactive debris.

Concussion Missile

We equipped your ship with standard AV42 Avenger concussion missiles. Since the Missile is a "dumb" weapon without any sophisticated guidance electronics, we anticipated no problems with the missile and you new Hyperdrive unit. Glad to see that we were right.

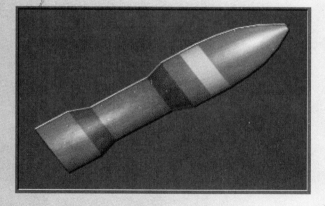

Your basic concussion missile may not be the latest in high tech gadgetry, but it packs a powerful punch and its high penetrative capacity made it a favorite in exploiting fissures when tunneling into bedrock within the mines. What that means to you, Material Defender, is that you should find more of this type of missile within the mines than any other. Also, the concussion missiles lack of bulky guidance electronics means that you can pack a full twenty of this type of Missile into your ship's weapons bay.

The concussion missile can be used against almost any foe at any range. Since the damage inflicted by the missile has a small burst radius at the impact point you can often damage several enemies at once.

Since the missile is unguided and fairly slow to accelerate towards it target you will have to take careful aim before firing. The only foe that this weapon is relatively ineffective against, therefore, are fast and maneuverable robots.

All missiles and mines inflict damage in a "burst" radius when they hit a target. This means that if you are too close to the target you will take damage as well. Make sure that your weapons are targeted far enough away so that you will not be included in the fun. Explosions are best enjoyed from a distance.

In addition, all missiles are set up to display what is directly in front of them. The missile-cam will be displayed in the lower right portion of your screen.

If you want to see what is in a room or far ahead of you. Launch a missile and look through its eyes. You may need to hold open a door for it with laser fire so that it can go through the door. This is a resource-expensive way to get a look around but can pay off for you when the need for information is vital.

Since you will be able to find these Missiles relatively easily within the mines you should become an expert in their effective use. Do not underestimate their usefulness, Material Defender.

Flash Missile

The flash missile was initially developed as a brighter replacement for your flares. The missile does negligible damage but has been modified to overload all sensors with a burst of both hot-bright light and a small electro-magnetic pulse. The light and the burst of energy seem to scramble the robot's sensors as well as it does human ones. The blinding effect caused by the missile lasts for only a few seconds.

Robots hit by a flash missile will usually continue to do whatever they were doing before they were hit by the flash missile. If they were firing at you they will continue to do so but they will not be able to track your movements until the Flash wears off. This weapon must be used in combination with other weapons to be of real use. Once a robot is blinded by a flash missile you must hurry to inflict maximal damage to it before it recovers. With larger and tougher robots this may mean that you will have to use several flash missiles— one every few seconds—to give you enough time to destroy your enemy.

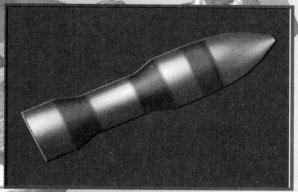

This special-purpose missile is ideal for use against solitary tough opponents at all ranges. It is less useful against groups of foes or smaller robots (because they can dodge it more readily).

Homing Missile

The NM35 Nemesis homing missile is a military upgrade of the venerable AV42 concussion missile. I deny any knowledge as to how these military-grade weapons came to be in the mines. Since they are there, you can make use of them. The robots will almost certainly use them against you.

The homing missile will attempt to home-in on any target that is within your sights when you fire the weapon (thereby activating its seeker-head). The homing missile cannot make extremely sharp turns (only up to about 45° or so) since its steering jets are quite small, but it is per-sistent. The homing missile has a larger warhead than the concussion missile and does more damage. Since the guidance electronics also take up more room, the homing missile is too bulky to allow you to squeeze more than ten into your weapons bay at any one time. Therefore, the weapon should be used with discre-tion. These weapons should be used for robots that are hard to hit with direct fire

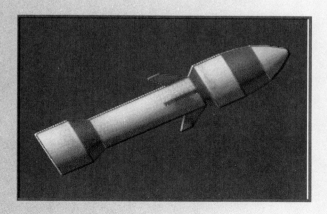

weapons or ones that you do not want to stand around and trade shots with because of their high damage-causing potential.

Since the weapon does not need active guiding by the pilot once it is fired (it is a 'fire and forget' weapon), you may fire the homing missile at a target and then duck safely out of sight behind cover.

Guided Missile

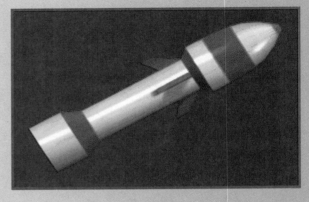

The guided missile uses advanced micro-scan technology and encoded burst transmitters to allow the pilot to actually fly this missile as though it were his own ship. The technology was actually developed to search for ore deposits in the asteroid belt. Several accidents with these probes prompted us to rework the flight controls. Here at R&D we have the greatest confidence that the actual cause for the probes turning around and locking-on to their own motherships was radiation from solar-flares. Deep in the mines you should have no problem with this anomalous loss of control. Why, we're almost completely certain.

The guided missile can be flown, for up to 30 seconds, as though it were your ship. If you fire another missile while you are flying a guided missile then the guided missile you are flying reverts to homing mode and will attempt to lock-on to the nearest enemy just as though it were a homing missile.

The guided missile can be controlled in two ways and each is best for different situations. The usual flight method is to use the small missile-cam view to fly the missile. The small missile viewscreen is set as the default. The advantage to this view is that it leaves the majority of your screen open to scan for new threats. The disadvantage is that the missile is somewhat harder to control using only the small screen. An option that gives you more control, but leaves your ship more vulnerable, is to turn the main viewscreen into the screen used for piloting the guided missile, leaving only the small screen to keep an eye on your ship. This gives you better vision for flying the Missile but leaves your ship more vulnerable since it is harder to see threats to your ship on the small screen.

To change the missile-cam view to full screen for firing the guided missile you must follow these steps; hit F2, select 'Options,' select 'Toggles,' and then select 'Show guided missile in Main Display.' Your viewscreens will now be swapped when you fire the guided missile (only).

Guided missiles are hard to find and should be reserved only for the toughest and hardest to hit targets. The guided missile is a good distance weapon since it can be flown for a full 30 seconds. It allows a pilot to position himself far away from enemy robots and fly the guided missile in to do the dirty work while your ship is safe, some distance away, preferably behind cover. Use these missiles wisely, Material Defender; they are the closest thing to a fighting wingman that you will have in the mines.

Proximity Bomb

The proximity bomb is a timed demolition charge that we have equipped with sensors. The net effect duplicates a military-grade area denial proximity bomb. We have tried to make this weapon as fool-proof as possible. Improperly used, however, this weapon is able to inflict massive damage to your own ship as well as to enemy robots.

Proper use protocol dictates that you drop the proximity bombs (either by triggering one of the secondary weapon buttons if you have the proximity bomb selected or by hitting B) and leave the area. We have designed your weapon bay so that you may drop the proximity bombs with equal safety moving either forward or in reverse. You have approximately two

seconds to leave the proximity of the bomb before it is armed. However, if the bomb is hit by enemy fire or an enemy ship within that initial arming-period, it will still explode. Drop the proximity bomb and move away from it. Rules to live by, Material Defender.

It's important to remember that if you are being fired upon or close-assaulted by robots you should probably not drop proximity bombs as they will almost certainly explode as soon as they leave your ship. This could easily cause enough damage to cripple or destroy your ship.

Also, proximity bombs will explode after approximately 30 seconds even without external prompting. Do not lurk around unexploded proximity bombs.

The proximity bomb is effective against robots through two different techniques. The first technique is to drop a cluster of several proximity bombs in such a way that you can lure enemy robots back towards you through the proximity bombs, forcing the robots to detonate the bombs. Robot generators are a first-class place to drop proximity bombs—provided you can do so between generation cycles. The second method is to drop proximity bombs near enemy robots and then turn around and shoot the proximity bombs with direct fire weapons as soon as enemy robots approach the bombs. The enemy robots should be caught in the blast of the exploding proximity bombs and will take damage even though they are not close enough to detonate the bombs themselves.

One further use of proximity bombs is to discourage tailgating. If you are being pursued nothing works better than a nice string of proximity bombs to stop tailgaters dead in their tracks. Just make sure that the pursuer is not close enough to catch you in the blast.

Smart Missile

The smart missile is one of the most versatile tools you have at your disposal for clearing a room of alien robots. The micro-technology used in the active homing plasma bomblets is a work of art. The unparalleled generosity of Sun-Ye Corporation in giving this vital technology to our research agents is extremely timely. You should find many more uses for the smart missile than you will be able to find actual missiles, Material Defender.

The smart missile is a large guided missile that does damage upon impact and releases a cluster of actively homing plasma bomblets. A direct hit with the smart missile causes massive damage. However, in addition to the initial explosion any enemy in the area will be targeted by one or more tiny bomblets of homing plasma released by the smart missile upon impact. Your ship will not be targeted no matter how close you are to the bomblets—an Identify Friend or Foe (IFF) transponder within each bomblet makes certain of that (although you can still be damaged by being too close to the initial impact explosion of the smart missile itself).

The smart missile can be used to shoot around corners. If you know that robots are waiting to pounce, just out of clear line of sight, a smart missile can be fired into a wall that would have a clear line of sight to the enemy. The smart missile will explode against the wall releasing the plasma bomblets to lock-on to any enemy ships that they can see from their release point.

The plasma bomblets released by the smart missile neither move nor turn fast, so if they must travel a long ways to reach their targets they may miss. Tactical doctrine for this weapon is to fire it into a small to mid-sized room (or other enclosed area) so that enemies do not have room to run or dodge the smart missile's plasma bomblets. Used in this way the smart missile can completely clear a room of smaller and less armored robots, or soften up a roomful of tougher opponents.

Mercury Missile

The Mercury missile was originally developed for rapid courier service. The Mercury missile uses a version of the Mercury Afterburner system (similar to the one available for your own ship). The Mercury missile flies faster than most direct-fire weapons and the payload,

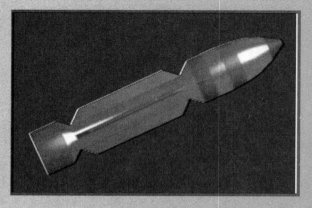

formerly used to carry important information and samples, now packs an impressive shaped-charge high-explosive punch. Although this missile has no room for bulky tracking avionics it flies fast enough for you to fire it just as easily as one of your ship's cannons.

Fast and powerful, this missile is the perfect weapon for large rooms and distant targets. It gets its message across before your opponent has time to run or dodge.

Mega Missile

The mega missile is one of the most powerful weapons in your arsenal, Material Defender. It was developed for fragmenting asteroids so that their debris could be harvested for ore. It's low yield nuclear warhead is capable of shattering almost anything that is small enough to be mobile. The active homing electronics are the very best currently available. The mega missile is very difficult to shake once it has locked on. When it does hit, most enemy robots will simply disappear in the blast and shockwave from this missile. The blast radius for this weapon is very large, and extreme caution must be used when firing the mega missile. Make certain that your ship is a safe distance away from the blast. Severe damage is inflicted by the mega missile out to a distance of several ship-lengths. The loss of your own ship is almost guaranteed if you use this weapon at point-blank range.

You will not find many of these ultra-powerful missiles within the mines. They are expensive to produce and dangerous to have around. Make sure that you save the mega missile for robots of the highest threat-level only. Do not squander your mega missiles on robots that can be more readily destroyed with lesser weapons. Save mega missiles for Boss robots and groups of the toughest foes. There are times when the proper use of a mega missile is your best chance to escape from a mine and if you're out of mega missiles, you may be just plain out of luck as well.

Many pilots have joked that these missiles should be painted with a 'have-a-nice-day' happy face on the nose. They reason is that the last thing an opponent sees should be something jovial to set the tone for their stay in the afterlife. Do not be on the receiving end of one of these missiles, Material Defender.

Shaker Missile

The shaker missile was originally designed to splinter smaller aster-oids (in the 50m to 100m range) for mineral harvesting. The shaker missile has a Mercury Afterburner system. This allows the missile to move far away from the firing ship as rapidly as possible. No tracking system is needed by the shaker missile as almost anything any-where near the impact point of the missile will be instantly vaporized. In fact only a very few of the toughest robots (i.e., Bosses) will remain after a detonation of one of these mis-siles. When the missile hits a target it releases several shockwaves and

also Multiple Independent Remote Vehicles (MIRVs or smaller sub-missiles) that do additional explosive damage to whatever they hit as they splinter off from the main impact point.

Use this extremely powerful weapon only against large accumulations of the toughest foes. This weapon will do severe damage to even the toughest Boss robots as well. Make certain that you only use this weapon at long range and when you are able to duck behind cover. Since the shaker missile releases MIRVs you must be clear of the blast zone and also clear of any potential sub-missiles that may come your way after the initial blast.

Tactical Summation

Your weapons are your key to surviving these missions, Material Defender. Your knowledge of the proper time and place to use each weapon will allow you to survive the rigors ahead. A lack of understanding of each weapon's advantages and disadvantages spells almost certain defeat and death within the bowels of one of the mines.

Study wisely and you may live, ignore these lessons and you will surely perish.

Besides, Material Defender, I've got a week's worth of pay riding on your making it through the first five mines. With the odds I'm getting—if you make it, I'm retiring a wealthy man.

Good luck, Material Defender.

Smith out.

<End Transmission>

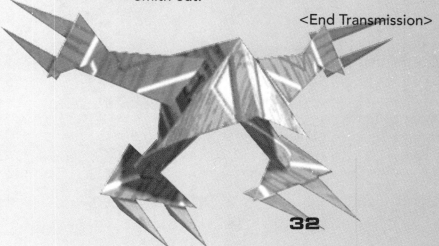

Mine Features

Status: Confidential

Transmission: 848.462.13 Fox-trot

To: Material Defender *in situ*

From: G. Cahn, Internal Security Forces, PTMC, Mines Division

CC: Dravis

Material Defender, Mr. Dravis has asked me to brief you on internal features of our mines. This information should prove useful to you. In fact, being unable to correctly identify the reactor cores that you need to destroy would cause your mission to be an utter failure. Therefore, I trust that you will find my information to be of the highest interest.

There are two types of objects that you can find within the mines. The first type are stationary mine features. The second are objects that your ship was designed to make use of. We call the non-stationary objects 'powerups' since they upgrade the abilities of your ship. In fact, many of these objects are also used by the robots and are interchangeable with your own ship's systems. Often you will be able to take some of these components from robots that you have destroyed. At other times you may find stockpiles of these objects floating in out of the way areas of the mines.

Since the mines have become infested some of the items that were originally within the mines have been altered somewhat. However, none of them should have been changed enough to be unrecognizable to you. Despite many heated memos written by me we did not have completely standardized equipment within the mines before the alien takeover.

Private memo #349

To: Dravis

Re: Standardization protocols within outer orbital mines

Mr. Dravis, as you may recall I insisted for months that we standardize our equipment within the mines. I would just like to go on record, again, by saying that if all of our switches and doors had been exactly the same then this whole infestation would never have happened. We would have immediately known just when the robots in the mines started to go wrong. This whole thing could have been prevented!

—G. Cahn

Reply- Dravis:

Of course, you must be right. I'll schedule a six month tour of inspections of our outer rim facilities for you this very afternoon. You will be able to catalog every single switch, in person. I'll make arrangements for you to leave just as soon as you write that report for me. Thank you, again, for bringing this matter to my attention.

—Dravis

Stationary Mine Features

Here are features of our mines that will be useful to you.

Energy Centers

The energy centers allow you to recharge your energy systems simply by flying through them. Your ship has receptors that are attuned to the frequency of energy created within the energy center's field of effect.

Each separate section within an energy center has a finite amount of energy available to recharge your ship. If you do exhaust one section of the energy center simply move to a different part of the center before attempting to recharge your ship's energy reserves.

Energy centers are designed to recharge mine robots rather than military craft. Because normal mining robots are built to lower tolerances the energy centers will not supercharge your energy supplies. Mine energy centers will only recharge your energy reserves up to 100 points rather than your ship's full 200 point capacity.

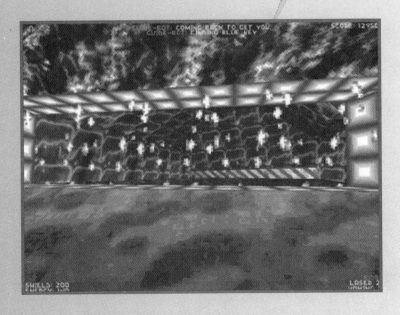

Robot Generator

Robot generating areas of the mines can be located almost anywhere. On your ship's automap they will appear as purple areas. Within the mines they will appear as a pulsing mass of purple lines when they are active. The purple lines are part of the robot generating station's power transference grid. While it is still capable of making new robots, the grid 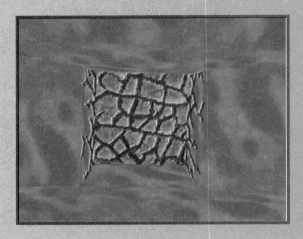 will pulse with energy. As soon as a robot generating station has exhausted its capacity to make new robots, the grid will stop glowing.

Robot generating areas are activated by your ship's presence. Many of them will reactivate every time you approach them.

They do have limitations, though. They are usually keyed to make only one or two different types of robot. Also, each robot generating center has a limited power reserve and they will eventually exhaust their ability to generate robots.

Switches

Many parts of the mine are activated by switches. Switches can be activated by shooting at them. This shorts out the switch and opens whatever the switch controlled.

Switches are sometimes located behind force-fields or grates. You may still trigger one of these switches by firing between the force-field or grate to destroy the switch. Also, not all switches look the same. Generally, if you are not certain whether something is a switch or not, just shoot it.

Each switch generally controls a door, or a wall section. Usually the affected area is adjacent to the activating switch. However, sometimes the

switch and the affected area are not adjacent. Most switches open areas that it would be beneficial for you to enter. Shooting switches is almost always a good strategy, but you must be prepared for ambush when you do so since many areas that switches open also contain enemy robots.

Keys

Another way to open doors is to use the special keys found within the mines. These keys are actually master-coded authorization transponders. When you pick up a colored key your ship will integrate the key's identifying frequency, which will allow you to enter any door that shares the key's color.

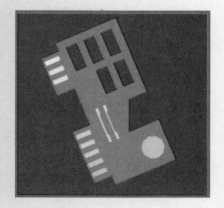

The keys allow access to progressive levels of security within each mine. You must use the blue key to reach each yellow key and the yellow key will allow access to the red key. The red key is used to gain final access to the reactor in each mine.

The aliens have recognized that defending access to the keys is an integral part of defending their mines. Keys are usually well defended, difficult to get to, or both. In fact, some keys are now being carried by robots and the carrying robot must be destroyed before the key can be retrieved.

Reactor

The reactor is the heart of each mine. When you destroy the reactor the mine will self-destruct. You will need the red key to enter each reactor area.

Each reactor may look slightly different as it is uniquely designed for each mine (for maximum efficiency). However, they are all easily identified by the pulsing plasma furnace within the containment field in the center of each reactor core, and also by the venting of some of the reactor's plasma towards your ship as part of its automated defense routine.

As soon as you destroy the reactor you must leave quickly as the energy normally processed by the reactor will build up within the mine until a complete meltdown occurs. The amount of time you have to safely escape depends upon the reactor and the mine's energy flow. The time may vary widely so know your escape route ahead of time if you can.

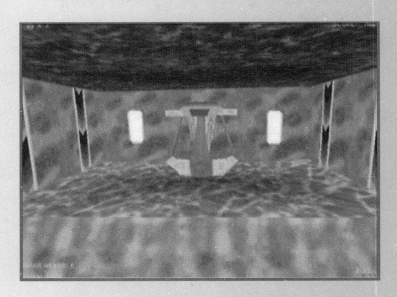

Force-fields

Force-fields are used within the mines to block access to hazardous or sensitive areas. Force-fields are usually turned off by a switch located somewhere nearby. Although, some force-fields cannot be turned off at all.

Force-fields reflect shots from energy weapons (including your Lasers). They will also do damage to your ship if you make contact with one. Your ship will rebound from contact with a force-field—be careful not to bounce into another force-field.

Powerups

The difficulty level that you select to fly through the mines determines the amount number of points that you get when you pick up a shield powerup or an energy powerup. The tougher the difficulty level, the fewer points you get from each powerup.

Energy Powerup

Energy powerups will add a variable amount of energy to your energy reserves. Energy gained from energy powerups can increase your energy higher than the normal 100 point limit (to a maximum of 200 points).

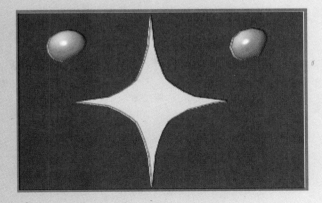

Shield Powerup

The shield powerup will replenish a variable amount of shield points to your ship's shields (up to a maximum limit of 200 points).

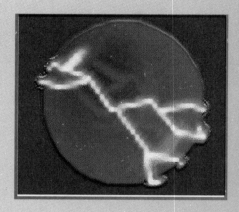

Energy/Shield Converter Powerup

The energy/shield converter powerup is a module that allows your ship to turn excess energy (Energy above 100 points) into shield points. Some energy is lost in the conversion process; your ship will gain half the energy points that you convert as shield points. You cannot increase your shield above 200 points using this process.

Headlight Powerup

The headlight powerup is a light that mounts to the front of your ship. It will illuminate the area in front of your ship. The powerful beam drains energy the entire time that it is on so you should use it only when absolutely necessary or you have easy access to more energy.

Cloaking Device Powerup

This device makes you invisible to robots. If you fire, the robots may attack the last position that you fired from but they cannot see your ship. Homing devices cannot track a cloaked ship.

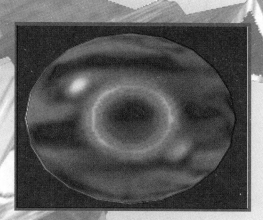

The cloaking device powerup only lasts for a limited amount of time, and you become cloaked as soon as you run over the powerup.

Afterburner Powerup

The afterburner powerup is a Mercury-style afterburner that can be field-fitted to your primary thrusters.

The afterburner doubles your forward speed for brief periods of time. As you use the afterburner the small red 'AB' bar in the cockpit view will lower. When the red is gone from this bar your afterburner must shut-off to replenish its energy reserves. Unlike your primary thruster engines, the afterburner costs energy to use. As soon as you stop using the after-burner, energy is shunted from your main power banks to the afterburner reserve and the red bar will automatically increase again (showing that you have a 'full-tank' of energy for the afterburner again). A full-tank of afterburner energy costs 10 energy points.

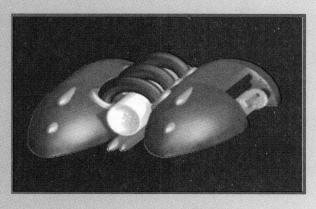

Additional Ship Powerup

The additional ship powerup grants access to reserve ships that have been secretly cached throughout the mines. This powerup adds one to the total of ships that you are able to use to complete your mission.

Map Powerup

The map powerup is a map card that integrates with your ships automapping system. The map powerup will allow you to see the entire mine in which it was found. The areas that are on your automap that you have not yet explored are shown in blue. Areas that you have actually been through are still shown in the usual white.

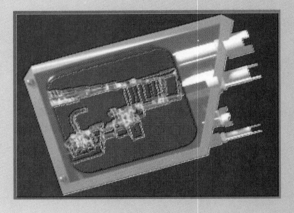

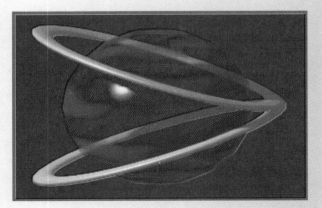

Invulnerability Powerup

The invulnerability powerup is an experimental shield device that renders your ship completely invulnerable to damage from any source for a brief period of time. The invulnerability starts automatically as soon as you fly over the powerup. Just before the powerup wears off, the shield surrounding the image of your ship in your cockpit view will flicker. Don't get yourself into trouble by allowing the invulnerability powerup to wear off while you are in a dangerous area.

I hope this information helps you, Material Defender. Most people just don't appreciate how important the nuts and bolts of mine construction are to adequate security.

G. Cahn, out.

<End Transmission>

Enemies

Status: Confidential

Transmission: 739.775.56 Zulu

To: Material Defender in situ

From: Dravis

Re: Tactical Appraisal of Robot OpFor per PTMC HQ Tactical Team

This is quite possibly the most important part of your briefing, Material Defender. I cannot tell you how this information was procured. I can tell you that it was not easy to come by. A wide variety of methods were used to gather this data as I believe this knowledge is vital to the success of the operation.

I hope you take the information to heart.

To aid you in recognition of your enemy, I have opted to provide you with both the technical nomenclature of the robots as well as the slang terms with which you may be more familiar. Think nothing of it, Material Defender; we only want to help you any way we can.

Each of the hostile robots have been analyzed in as much detail as possible. The information that we have on each one has been gone over by our top tactical advisors. Top men, Material Defender.

Each robot's attack pattern and the tactics thought most likely to be of success against it will be detailed for you in the briefing that follows. Each has been listed with its relative Threat index (a combination of

weaponry and aggressiveness), its Armor rating, and its Maneuverability (a combination of both speed and turning ability). These ratings should help you in danger evaluation procedures.

When there are special tactics that offer a high likelihood of success against a particular type of robot, these will be mentioned as well.

Guidebot

PTMC Coding: Guidebot

Threat: None

Armor: Heavy

Maneuverability: High

This robot is the only friendly robot that you will find in the mines. The Guidebot was originally designed to acquire information on the status of mine projects and to assist supervisors in finding problem areas within each mine. As a result of this the Guidebot's ability to find specified objects or areas is unparalleled. Your ship is equipped with the necessary command codes so that you may use the Guidebot to help you during your mine insertions.

The Guidebot is usually housed within each mine somewhere near the entrance to the mine. This design was so that supervisors would be able to access the Guidebot soon after entering the mine.

In order to start making use of the Guidebot, and to be able to issue commands to it, you must first release the it by shooting away the door-grate that closes in its storage hangar.

If you don't assign the Guidebot a task it will start on its supervisor-inspection routine. This consists of touring the mines key by key. To bring up a list of tasks that you can assign the Guidebot to follow depress [Shift] and [F4] at the same time.

The Guidebot can also serve as a scout for you. The other robots in the mines will ignore the Guidebot since it too is a robot. To use the Guidebot as a spy, depress [Shift] and either [F1] or [F2]. This will cycle different views through your small camera windows. The second view should say 'Guidebot.' This will show you what your Guidebot sees. You can't really control where your Guidebot looks but with patience and a little luck you can use the Guidebot to scout out your upcoming route.

The Guidebot can take damage from your shots. It is a very durable design but is not indestructible. If you are shooting your Guidebot it will let you know by broadcasting an 'Ouch' message.

Use your Guidebot well, Material Defender, it will be the closest thing to a wingman that you will have during your missions.

Bluefly

PTMC Coding: Portable Equalizing Standard Transbot (PEST)

Threat: Low

Armor: Light

Maneuverability: High

The Bluefly is a small scout robot. It is more of a nuisance than a threat but occasionally it will attempt to lure unsuspecting pilots into an ambush.

The best way to fight the Bluefly is by staying at long range. It's rapid-fire pulse laser is extremely inaccurate at long range and so it can be engaged with relative safety.

Salamander

PTMC Coding: Internal Tactical Droid

Threat: Low

Armor: Light

Maneuverability: Medium

The Salamander is a versatile, light scout robot that shoots small, low power plasma

balls. Alone, the Salamander is not much of a threat and it falls more into the nuisance category. However, when encountered in groups the Salamander can be dangerous. The aliens use this extremely versatile robot with a number of camouflage patterns as a sniper-robot. The Salamander is often used as a mine-laying robot, and many camouflaged Salamanders are mine-layers. In mine-laying mode the main armament has been replaced by mine dropping equipment.

Minotaur

PTMC Coding: Preliminary Interogation Robot (PIG)

Threat: Low

Armor: Medium

Maneuverability: Low

The Minotaur is a medium sized robot with good armor for its size. It is a tenacious foe but slow and not very maneuverable. The Minotaur is armed with a pair of medium strength lasers.

Thiefbot

PTMC Coding: Bandit

Threat: High

Armor: Extremely Heavy

Maneuverability: High

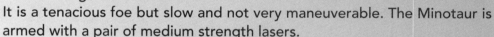

The Thiefbot is a heavily-modified rubbish collection robot. In order to get clear of hazardous areas within the mines, the original rubbish collection robot was made quick and extremely agile. The Thiefbot retains those qualities and has added the virtue of extreme toughness. The lack of offensive armament allows the Thiefbot to move faster and carry far more armor than most robots its size.

The Thiefbot will attempt to close and to steal a weapon from you. Its claws are designed so that it has to do little more than touch your ship to accomplish this. It will be deterred by weapons fire but will return to try to your selected weapons as soon as you stop firing at it.

The best tactic to destroy the Thiefbot is to find a long corridor and to fire at the Thiefbot as it approaches your ship down the length of the 'killing-zone' that you have set up. The Thiefbot takes a lot of damage to kill so this tactic will take a while to be successful, but the only other alternative is to continue through the mines with the Thiefbot continually stealing whatever weapon you have selected.

The Thiefbot can only steal weapons that have been added to your ship, it cannot take your initial (level one) lasers.

Spartan

PTMC Coding: Smelter

Threat: Medium

Armor: Medium

Maneuverability: Low

The Spartan is used throughout the mines as a standard foot-soldier robot. It uses twin Phoenix Cannons as its primary armament. This means that the Spartan's bouncing shots can hit you even when you would be safely behind cover for most direct fire weapons.

The Spartan is another robot that is often used for camouflaged-sniper and mine-laying duties.

The Spartan can be out-turned by a good pilot. Try to slide to the Spartan's side to shoot at it from a position that does not allow it to return fire.

DESCENT II The Official Strategy Guide

Fire Snail

PTMC Coding: no
information available

Threat: Low

Armor: Medium

Maneuverability: Low

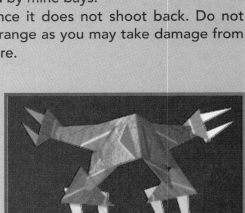

The Fire Snail is a mine-laying version of the Spartan. It is usually camouflaged a deep red color and has had its phoenix cannons replaced by mine bays.

This robot is easy to destroy since it does not shoot back. Do not shoot at this robot from too close a range as you may take damage from recently dropped mines hit by your fire.

Grizzly

PTMC Coding: Diamond
Claw

Threat: High

Armor: High

Maneuverability: Medium

The Grizzly was once an advanced heavy-lifter robot. The strong claws that once enabled the Grizzly to lift and crunch rocks with ease are now used against your ship, Material Defender.

The Grizzly is a clever and resourceful foe and will attempt to use stealth to sneak up close enough to use its hardened claws.

The aliens have added active armor to the Grizzly's formidable combat abilities. The active armor used by the Grizzly fires one or more rounds of homing plasma at the nearest target (you) whenever the Grizzly is struck by weaponry.

48

Fight the Grizzly at long range if you can. At close range it will use its claws to deadly effect and you will not have enough time or space to dodge its homing plasma. Shooting the Grizzly with the gauss gun, vulcan cannon, or missiles will defeat its active armor.

Sidearm

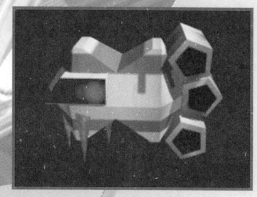

PTMC Coding: Sidearm

Threat: Medium

Armor: Heavy

Maneuverability: Low

The Sidearm is a large, bulky, and slow robot that was once used for heavy drilling supervision. It now has two weapons systems. The Sidearm fires both flash missiles and shaped-plasma star shot.

The Sidearm has a fair amount of armor but also poor maneuverability.

Out-turn this big slug in order to destroy it. When you do destroy it, though, it will release several small Flashbots (see below). Much of the time, the same shots that kill the Sidearm will destroy some, or all, of the newly released Flashbots. Try to kill only Sidearm at a time or you may end up with a room full of Flashbots.

Flashbot

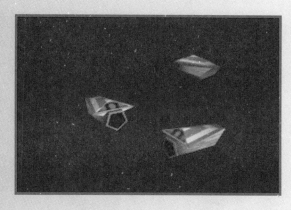

PTMC Coding: Sidearm Modula

Threat: Low

Armor: Light

Maneuverability: High

The tiny Flashbot was once used to illuminate work areas

and to serve as a remote scout for the larger Sidearm robot. Alone, Flashbots are little cause for concern, but they usually operate in small groups and tend to attack when you are already fending off other enemies.

Several hits by the flash missiles that are the Flashbots only weapon will leave you blind and defenseless in the face of attacks by more dangerous foes.

Centurion

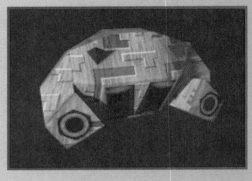

PTMC Coding: Lou Guard

Threat: High

Armor: Heavy

Maneuverability: Medium

The Centurion is an extremely deadly enemy. Originally designed for long-range perimeter defense, the Centurion is an excellent hunter-killer robot. It is aggressive and fires two homing missiles at once. It carries heavy armor, and while it is not fast, it can turn with surprising agility.

This robot is difficult to outmaneuver and much of your time fighting it should be spent dodging the many homing missiles that it can throw at you. Perseverance and caution are the means to defeating this foe.

Triton

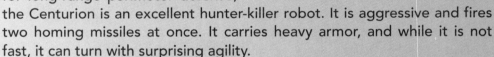

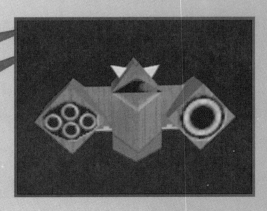

PTMC Coding: Internal Tactical Security Robot

Threat: Medium

Armor: Medium

Maneuverability: Medium

The Triton was designed as a heavier scout robot than the Bluefly, although it shares many traits with its smaller cousin. The Triton is some-what aggressive but will retreat if pressed. It is armed with two rapid-fire pulse lasers which lack long-range accuracy. However, the Triton also has a concussion missile system which does enable it to be somewhat effective at longer ranges.

The Triton's cleverness at retreating will not help it in the face of a determined attack. Consistently attack this robot and it will soon wither before your guns.

Blue Crab

    PTMC Coding: Fox Attack Robot

    Threat: Medium

    Armor: Medium

    Maneuverability: Medium

The Blue Crab robot was once used to sort through ore deposits. It is not a particularly diffi-cult opponent to overcome but there are many of them since they were once used in great numbers throughout the mines.

The Blue Crab is armed with a two-barrel blue plasma gun. It has claw arms but they are designed for sorting, not digging, and are too weak to effect your ship as a weapon.

Brain

    PTMC Coding: no
        information available

    Threat: Variable

    Armor: Heavy

    Maneuverability: Low

The Brain bot does not attack or cause damage by itself. However,

DESCENT II The Official Strategy Guide

when one of these robots is around, all other robots in the immediate vicinity will fight more intelligently. That is why there is a variable threat level assigned to this robot. The danger it represents is entirely dependent upon which robots it is able to personally direct.

If you can, you should always attempt to take out this foe first.

War Helm

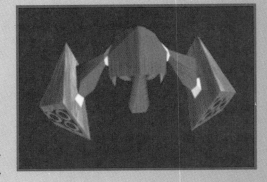

PTMC Coding: Seeker

Threat: High

Armor: Heavy

Maneuverability: Medium

The War Helm is a dangerous foe. The Mercury missiles that the War Helm is armed with are extremely difficult to dodge since they move faster than laser shots and can cause quite a bit of damage with each hit. The War Helm is also heavily armored so it can continue firing even when your most potent weapons are brought to bear upon it.

Try not to assault this robot head on. Moving in close can be an effective tactic with this robot as long as you continue to slide around the robot to keep it from facing you to fire. At long ranges, duck frequently as you approach the War Helm. You may not even see the missiles until they are too close to dodge.

Bulldog

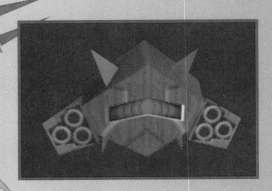

PTMC Coding: Bulk Destroyer

Threat: Medium

Armor: Medium

Maneuverability: Medium

The Bulldog was designed as a quick driller robot designed to make blast-bores with its two vulcan cannons. This robot will often engage you at long range, sometimes before you can even see it. It is fond of hiding in dark corners of large rooms and sniping at you. It will also engage aggressively at close range as well.

The Bulldog needs to be taken out fast and you will probably need to close with it in order to do so since the Bulldog's twin vulcans give it a tangible advantage at long range.

Kamikaze

PTMC Coding: Omega Defense Spawn

Threat: High

Armor: Medium

Maneuverability: Very High

The Kamikaze robot was originally designed as a remote explosive charge. It has one goal. It wants to run into your ship and blow itself up. It's high speed and maneuverability (easily the most maneuverable ship in the mines) make it a difficult opponent to stop.

Its speed and small size make this an ideal robot to use as a mine-layer and the robot will often be camouflaged and converted for use in that role.

Distance is your best defense. Try to stay as far away as possible as you shoot at this robot to detonate it before it succeeds in closing with you.

Mosquito

PTMC Coding: Ice Spindle Defense Robot

Threat: Medium

Armor: Medium

Maneuverability: Medium

This is another ore sorting and general processing robot that the aliens have pressed into service as a

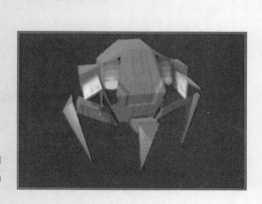

DESCENT II The Official Strategy Guide

mine guard. The Mosquito's long legs are too narrow for use as weapons but the robot is equipped with twin blue plasma launchers.

Gnat and Super Gnat

PTMC Coding: Red Hornet and Spawn

Threat: Low

Armor: Light

Maneuverability: High

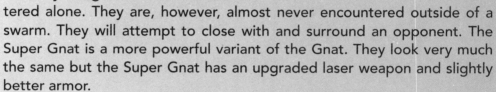

The Gnat and the Super Gnat are not very dangerous when encountered alone. They are, however, almost never encountered outside of a swarm. They will attempt to close with and surround an opponent. The Super Gnat is a more powerful variant of the Gnat. They look very much the same but the Super Gnat has an upgraded laser weapon and slightly better armor.

Gnats are released by the Brood Spider robot when the Brood Spider is destroyed.

Star Spider

PTMC Coding: BPER Bot

Threat: Medium

Armor: Light

Maneuverability: High

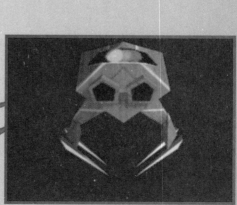

The Star Spider is an alien war robot. It is very maneuverable for its size. It fires a shaped-charge plasma star shot and has a high rate of fire. Beware of this when attacking it. Direct fire weapons have a better chance against this robot as it is maneuverable enough to avoid most missiles fired at it.

Tiger

PTMC Coding: no information available

Threat: High

Armor: Very Heavy

Maneuverability: Low

The Tiger is a heavy attack robot. It has three primary weapons systems with two shaped plasma star-shot launchers and on homing missile launcher.

Patience is needed when fighting this opponent. The Tiger absorbs so much punishment that it is almost impossible to destroy a Tiger in one attack run.

Energy Wasp

PTMC Coding: E-Bandit

Threat: Medium

Armor: Heavy

Maneuverability: Medium

The Energy Wasp was originally designed to patrol the mines to find and dissipate excess electrical buildups. The Energy Wasp has claws that it uses to grasp and then generate a field that dissipates electrical energy. The robot has been reprogrammed to use this ability against intruders.

The Energy Wasp will attempt to close as rapidly as possible and then will push your ship back as it claws you with its grappling claws. The field generated by the claws will leach energy from your ship at the same time.

The best defense against a charging opponent like the Energy Wasp is to give ground as it charges. This tactic will give you more time to

shoot at it and hopefully destroy it before it starts to suck precious energy from your ship.

Red Mantis

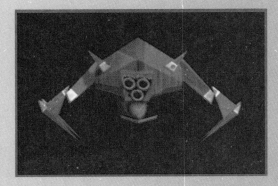

PTMC Coding: TRN Racer

Threat: Medium

Armor: Medium

Maneuverability: Medium

The Red Mantis was originally designed for exploratory mining. It has a large sensor eye and both drilling and handling equipment. The triple fire plasma ball weapon was originally intended for use as a drill and the claws work as well on composite armor as they did on stone.

The Mantis is not very eager to close to use its claws unless the player turns their back on it. The best way to fight his robot is to press the attack slightly. By moving towards the Red Mantis you should keep it backing away from you and that will limit its offense to only the Plasma burst weapon.

Brood Spider

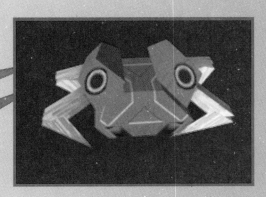

PTMC Coding: Spider

Threat: Medium

Armor: Low

Maneuverability: Medium

The Brood Spider is an alien robot that serves as a carrier for Gnats and Super Gnats. The Brood

Spider always has a full load of Gnats on board and will expel them if destroyed. The Brood Spider is extremely aggressive and has little concern for its own safety. Its sole concern is to sink its twin concussion missile fangs into you before it dies.

As with the Sidearm robot, a good kill-shot will often take out some of the Brood Spider's dangerous cargo as well as the Brood Spider itself. Try to destroy this robot at a distance or you will be overwhelmed by its Gnat cargo.

Green Dragon

PTMC Coding: Boarshead

Threat: High

Armor: Medium

Maneuverability: Low

The Green Dragon is a hybrid alien robot. It appears to have been designed around the cores of a drilling robot and a defense robot since one of its weapons is a mining tool (the plasma cannon is a drilling tool) and the other is more often a long range weapon (the smart missile is not usually used for mining).

The flexibility in this arrangement makes good sense, unfortunately. At close to medium ranges the plasma cannon will lock onto a foe, and at longer ranges the missile is more effective. Of course, at mid-ranges your ship is at risk from both sources. A favorite tactic of the Green Dragon is to engage you with the plasma cannon and then to fire the smart missile behind you so that the plasma bomblets (contained in the smart missile) burst behind you. You can't dodge what you can't see—you get caught between a rock and the proverbial hard place.

Fortunately, this robot is not particularly maneuverable, nor is it extremely well armored. Just try to keep aware of where its smart missiles are going as you concentrate your fire on it.

Alien Mines

While this is not exactly an alien robot, it is an alien device and it is dangerous. The Alien Mine is a very potent high explosive device. It is much smaller than our own mine and does much more damage. The aliens are fond of placing

these in dangerous spots and natural choke-points.

Places to look for these include darkened corridors, dropshafts, behind doors, and in any place where an ambush may be set-up.

The Aliens never place their mines singly. If you have found one, there are sure to be more.

Mine-Boss Robots

These are one of a kind 'Command' robots that control entire mines and coordinate the power supply of the mines that they control (since mines that have Mine-Boss robots do not have Reactors). Destroying one of these Bosses shuts down a mine in the same way that destroying the mine's Reactor would normally.

There are six Mine-Boss (or simply Boss) robots that you will meet within the mines. Each one has a different weapons system but the basic capabilities of each Boss robot are very similar.

The Boss robot ability to monitor and conduct power transfers limits their range within each mine to only one large room. Each Boss robot is extremely well armored. Also, the Boss robots have the ability to teleport to other parts of their room. When the Boss is ready to teleport it becomes translucent. But this teleportation ability is not instantaneous—as long as you can see the Boss you can still inflict damage to it. Even when the image of the Boss begins to disappear, weapons fired at the Boss will still produce impact explosions. Finally, each Boss is very well armed.

Since each Boss shares very similar, dangerous, qualities, the methods used to defeat the Boss robots is the same from Boss to Boss.

The first thing to remember when fighting a Boss is that it will be a long fight. You cannot trade blows with one of the Mine-Bosses. Most are able to shrug off any single hit (even from a shaker missile). You must continually hit and run. This is made doubly important by the fact that you never know what part of the room the Boss is going to reappear in after teleporting. Keep moving, never sit still.

When you see the Boss, fire a shot or two and then run. When you run, do not run in a straight line. Almost every Boss has some kind of homing weapon. In order to survive you must run and then duck quickly around a corner so that any homing munitions that the Boss has fired at you will pass harmlessly by. This usually takes some time and, if performed well, can be likened to some sort of macabre minuet.

Mine Boss for Mine 4

This Mine Boss is the lightest armed and armored that you will encounter. It is armed with two homing missile launchers.

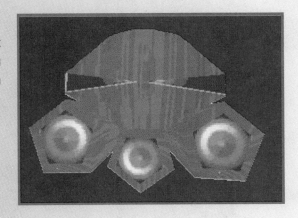

Mine Boss for Mine 8

This Mine Boss is very elusive. It is armed with two Mercury missile launchers and one smart mine dispenser. It will often try to attack from a distance with the Mercury missiles and also will detonate its own mines shortly after laying them in order to catch your ship unawares with this somewhat unusual attack.

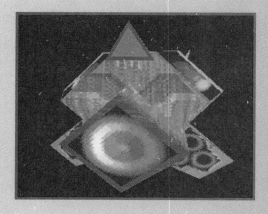

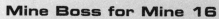

Mine Boss for Mine 12

This Mine Boss fires three phoenix cannons and a mega missile. It is particularly adept at banking its phoenix cannon shots off walls to hit you with indirect fire. Also, with its mega missile launcher this is the first Boss with a weapon that can kill you with one shot. Hopefully, Material Defender, you will have perfected your dodge by the time you must face this monster.

Mine Boss for Mine 16

This Mine Boss is equipped with an omega cannon and flash missiles. It will try to blind you with the Flash Missiles and then come in close for the coup-de-grace with the short range omega cannon. Even if you have been blinded by flash missiles, keep moving.

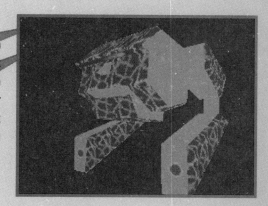

Mine Boss for Mine 20

This Boss has dual launchers for Mercury missiles. The number of Mercury Missiles that this Boss can pump-out at a foe is incredible. A high rate of fire and the speedy rate of the missiles themselves make this boss a foe to be respected.

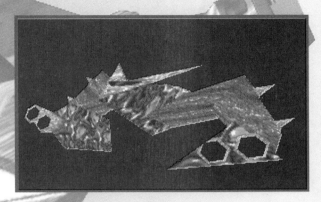

Mine Boss for Mine 24

The last known alien mine contains the very nastiest of the Mine Bosses. This Boss fires shaker missiles two at a time from twin wing mounts. This foe must be fought very tenaciously and carefully in order to survive its devastating attacks.

PART 2

MISSION
MAPS

Map Key Codes

X represents your insertion point.

Weapons and other objects found within the mines will be designated by letters and indicated by circles on the maps as follows:

WEAPONS AND POWERUPS

Letter	Object
AP	Ammunition Powerup
B	Proximity Bomb
CM	Concussion Missile
CP	Cloaking Device Powerup
DP	Additional-Ship Powerup
EM	Mega Missile
EP	Energy Powerup
FC	Fusion Cannon
FM	Flash Missile
GC	Gauss Cannon
GM	Guided Missile
HC	Helix Cannon
HM	Homing Missile
HP	Headlight Powerup
IP	Invulnerability Powerup
KM	Shaker Missile
LP	Laser Powerup
M	Smart Mines
MM	Mercury Missile
MP	Map Powerup
OC	Omega Cannon
PC	Plasma Cannon
QP	Quad Laser Powerup
RP	Ammunition Rack Powerup
SC	Spreadfire Cannon
SE	Shield/Energy Converter
SM	Smart Missile
SP	Shield Powerup
UP	Super-Laser Powerup
VC	Vulcan Cannon
VP	Afterburner Powerup
XC	Phoenix Cannon

ADDITIONAL MINE FEATURES

+	Switch
*	Secret Level Entrance
D	Door
EC	Energy Center
RG	Robot Generator
S	Secret Door

Robots are designated by 2-letter codes and indicated by squares on the maps as follows:

ROBOTS

Letters	Robot Name
AM	Alien Mines
BC	Blue Crab
BD	Bulldog
BF	Bluefly
BR	Brain
BS	Brood Spider
CT	Centurion
EW	Energy Wasp
FL	Flashbot
FS	Fire Snail
GB	Guidebot
GD	Green Dragon
GN	Gnat
GR	Grizzly
KA	Kamikaze
MI	Minotaur
MQ	Mosquito
RD	Red Mantis
SA	Sidearm
SG	Super Gnat
SL	Salamander
SR	Spartan
SS	Star Spider
TG	Tiger
TH	Thiefbot
TR	Triton
WH	War Helm

Note: Cloaked robots are underlined.

Mine 1—Ahayweh Gate

Just to your right as you start is the Guidebot, caged inside a cell. Free it if you want its help, but it's not necessary for this level.

Fly forward and bear to the left of your starting position until you are facing a red door. To the left of the red door is a corridor that slopes downward; take it straight down, ignoring all side passages. At the bottom of the corridor is a large chamber with two doors. You want the one to the left of the chamber entrance that reads "Weapons Testing Area." Open the door and fly directly to the opposite side of the chamber where the red key is floating. Snag the key and leave by the door you came in.

Once back in the large chamber, bear to the right and head back up the sloping corridor you used to enter the chamber (the corridor will be marked with black and yellow construction hatching around the opening for easy identification). Stop at the top of the corridor at the red door and open it. Fly into the room beyond and go into the (seemingly) dead-end corridor at the bottom of the chamber opposite the entrance. Shoot the panels on either side of the dead end then fly through the open door that is revealed. Beyond is the reactor: Destroy it and make for the exit.

Once you have destroyed the reactor, fly up to the top of the room, turn your back on the exploding reactor, and fly through the exit. Let the dying reactor choke on your vapor trail.

Congratulations! You have finished the Ahayweh Gate, your first *Descent 2* mission.

Mine 2—Turnabout Bore

This level is complicated by the arrival of a new robot, a Spartan. Slow and ponderous, however, they are not much of a threat.

You start facing the only exit. Open the exit door and enter the secondary chamber. You will see two doors in this room. There is also a Guidebot imprisoned in the cage on the floor of the room.

Shoot the panel by the unmarked door to the left. Open the door and fly down the large corridor that is revealed. Just past the laser recharge area to the right is a door marked "Warning: Low Gravity." Open the door, fly down the corridor to the hub chamber, then up and out the opposite corridor.

At the top of the corridor is a door. Shoot it open and bear right into the second large corridor. At the end of this long corridor is a room with a lava floor. Floating in the middle is the blue key. Grab it and get out.

Once you have the blue key, retrace your flight path: Leave the blue key room, flying back down the large corridor until you reach the door you entered from. Open it, proceed down the corridor, through the hub chamber, and back up and out the opposite corridor. Open the door, bear left past the laser recharge area until you are back in the room with the Guidebot.

Take the only remaining door (marked "Humans Only Beyond this Point") and go down the corridor. Shoot open the blue access door at the end. Enter the large corridor, bearing right. You will pass a laser recharge door on the right, a robot recharge area above it, and more importantly, the red door on the left (marked "Weapons Testing Area" as on the Ahayweh Gate). Make a note of it, then proceed to the end of the large corridor. On the left will be a door marked "Danger: Radiation." Open the door, proceed through the first red room to the door on the opposite side, then into the chamber beyond.

Once you have entered this chamber, bear right along the wall: There is a door to the right of the entrance. Open it, then follow the four red curving chambers all the way to the end where two purple robots guard a door. Open the door, then bear left into the large corridor beyond. Follow the path along the lava floor until you reach a door at the end. Open it and shoot the panel directly in front of you (this will prevent the door from locking behind you), then descend into the corridor beyond. Watch out for the robot generator beneath the door. At the end of the corridor to the left is the red key, encased by a force field.

Once you reach the force field, you will have to practice some precision shooting—shoot between the force field beams to open a secret door behind the red key. Shoot the panel that is revealed. This will shut down the force field, but it will also cause secret doors to open to the

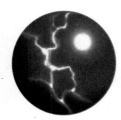

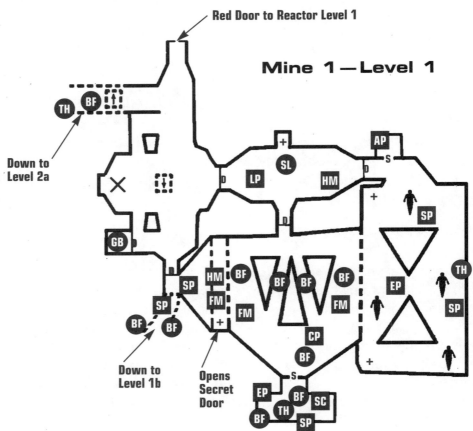

Red Door to Reactor Level 1

Mine 1—Level 1

TH BF

Down to
Level 2a

+

SL

AP
S

D

LP

HM

D

+

SP

GB

SP

HM

BF

BF

BF

BF

FM

TH

FM

FM

EP

SP

SP

BF

BF

Down to
Level 1b

+

CP

BF

+

Opens
Secret
Door

S

EP

BF
SC

BF

TH

SP

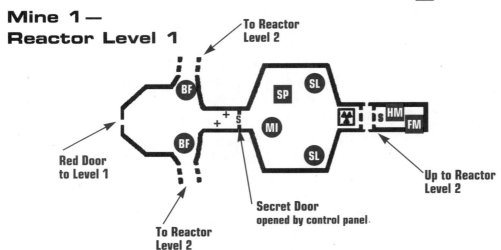

Mine 1—
Reactor Level 1

To Reactor
Level 2

BF

SP

SL

+

S

HM

Red Door
to Level 1

BF

MI

FM

+

SL

Up to Reactor
Level 2

Secret Door
opened by control panel.

To Reactor
Level 2

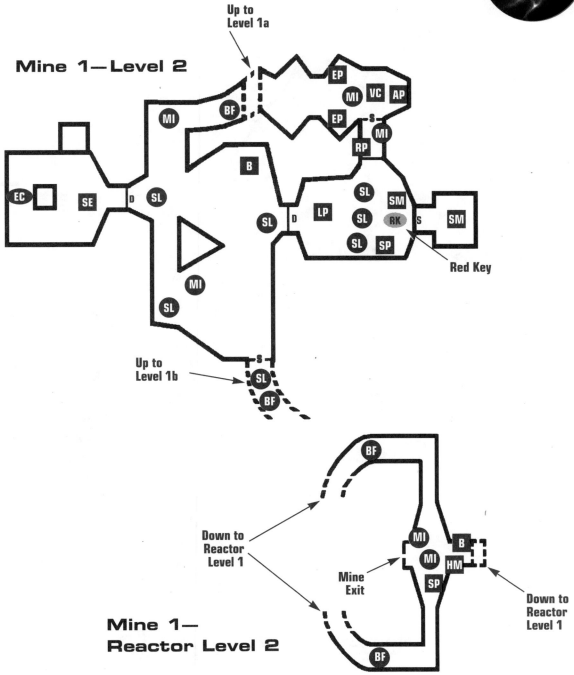

Mine 1—Level 2

Up to
Level 1a

Up to
Level 1b

Red Key

**Mine 1—
Reactor Level 2**

Down to
Reactor
Level 1

Mine
Exit

Down to
Reactor
Level 1

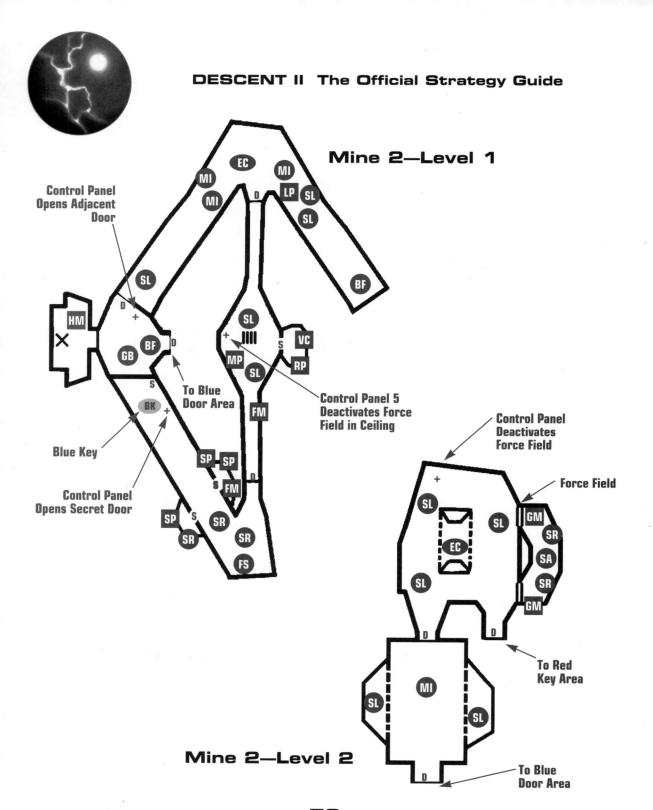

Mine 2—Level 1

Control Panel
Opens Adjacent
Door

Control Panel 5
Deactivates Force
Field in Ceiling

To Blue
Door Area

Blue Key

Control Panel
Opens Secret Door

Control Panel
Deactivates
Force Field

Force Field

To Red
Key Area

Mine 2—Level 2

To Blue
Door Area

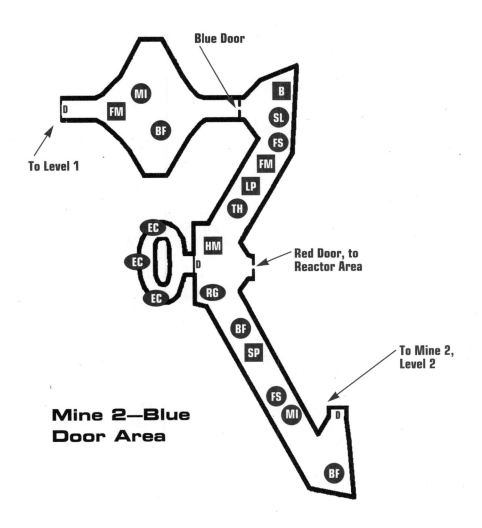

Blue Door

MI

FM

BF

D

To Level 1

B

SL

FS

FM

LP

TH

EC

EC

EC

HM

D

RG

Red Door, to
Reactor Area

BF

SP

To Mine 2,
Level 2

FS

MI

D

Mine 2—Blue
Door Area

BF

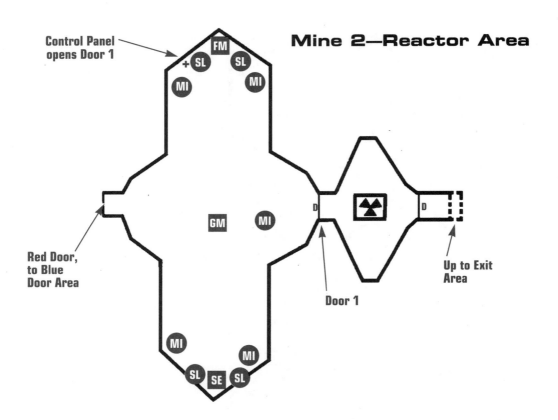

Mine 2—Reactor Area

Control Panel opens Door 1

Red Door, to Blue Door Area

Door 1

Up to Exit Area

PART 2   Mission Maps

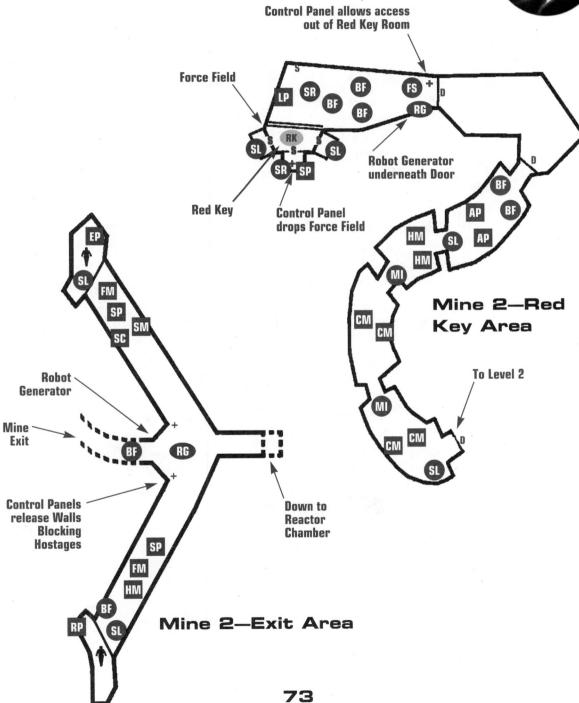

Control Panel allows access out of Red Key Room

Force Field

Robot Generator underneath Door

Red Key

Control Panel drops Force Field

Mine 2—Red Key Area

To Level 2

Robot Generator

Mine Exit

Control Panels release Walls Blocking Hostages

Down to Reactor Chamber

Mine 2—Exit Area

sides and behind you, spilling out more robot attackers. Rush in, grab the red key and get out.

Time to backtrack: Head back down the corridor, fly up to the door, open it, then follow the lava floor of the corridor back to the door on the right you entered from (again, it will be marked "Humans Only Beyond this Point"). Fly back through the four red curving chambers to the room with the two force fields. Follow the wall of the room to the left and open the door. Fly through the small red chamber and re-enter the large corridor, bearing right. Fly down and shoot open the red access door to your right (again, watch out for the robot generator in the upper left of the corridor).

You'll enter a large room with a bridge spanning a lava floor. Shoot the panel to the bottom left of the chamber. This will open the door on the opposite side of the room, allowing you access to the reactor.

After you destroy the reactor, fly into the corridor behind it. Follow the glowing red line up and over to where it ends in a door. Open the door to enter the large corridor beyond, but watch out for the robot generator on the floor! The exit door lies on the opposite side of the large corridor. Take it and leave the Turnabout Bore.

Mine 3—Wenl Mine

The Wenl Mine on Zeta Aquilae 3 poses no new challenges, but does force you to utilize the skills you have already developed even further. Upon entry to the mine, you appear in a chamber with numerous powerups and no immediate threats.

Immediately leading out of this room is a door opening up to a large chamber with two robot generators recessed into the ceiling. They do not become active when you enter, but you still face opposition in the form of Blueflies, Minotaurs, Salamanders, and a Grizzly.

Take care as the path to the blue key is littered with these and additional Spartans. The best tactic here is to maximize available cover and knock each robot out one by one, while being careful not to let yourself be ambushed by the Thief-bot.

The blue key chamber itself is guarded by similar robots which have plenty of available cover in the alcoves. Sniping from the doorway is the safest method of eliminating these guardians.

Once you have the blue key, take great care as you retrace your steps back to the large central chamber and the blue door. Along the way you will encounter many robots that have emerged from behind hidden doors that opened when you retrieved the key. Double back slowly, and eliminate your opposition one robot at a time until the way is clear.

Back in the main chamber, there is stiff opposition as the robot generators come to life. Sniping from behind cover works best here since there are too many robots between you and the blue door. Also, the entry way to this door has been mined, so using afterburners to sidestep your way past robots will only get you killed. Clear out this room slowly and carefully.

On the way up to level two are two Minotaurs ready to ambush you, but the chamber in level two should be clear of immediate threats. En route to the yellow key you may find little opposition, but be aware that robots often are lying in wait within alcoves.

In the red key room the entrance will guarded by a variety of robots, including Spartans. Be careful not to let them pin you down in an alcove, since their phoenix cannons will pulverize whatever shields you may have remaining. Once the room is clear of robots, you will notice that the red key is trapped behind a force-field. This force-field can be easily knocked out by destroying the control panel behind the red key.

The Reactor Chamber is a little tricky since there is a robot generator next to the reactor core, and it will activate when you get close. The safest tactic, unless you are completely confident about your maneuvering skills, is to blow the reactor from maximum distance and cover—using a quad-laser if possible.

When the reactor is destroyed, race back to where the yellow key was located and you will find the mine exit in the ceiling. Beware, multiple Grizzlies will be released from hidden doors as soon as you make your approach . . .

Mine 3—Level 1

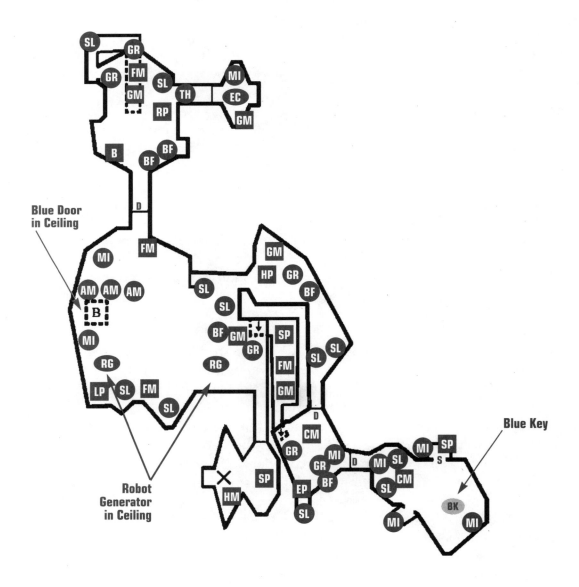

Blue Door
in Ceiling

Robot
Generator
in Ceiling

Blue Key

Mine 3—Level 2

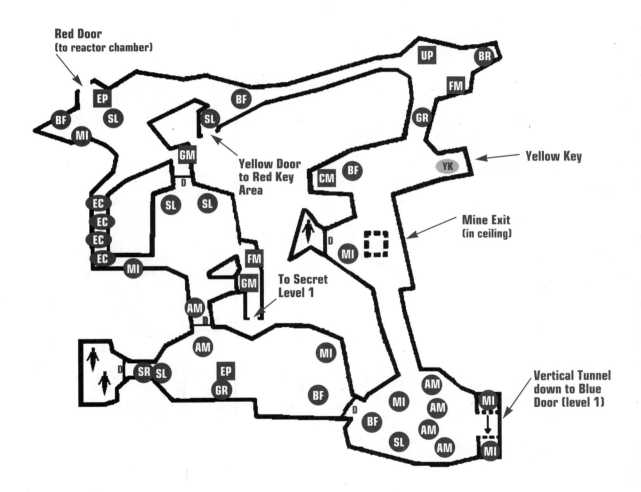

Red Door
(to reactor chamber)

EP

BF

SL

BF

MI

GM

D

SL

SL

EC
EC
EC
EC
EC

MI

BF

SL

Yellow Door
to Red Key
Area

CM

BF

YK   ←   Yellow Key

UP

BR

FM

GR

D

MI

Mine Exit
(in ceiling)

FM

GM

To Secret
Level 1

AM

AM

MI

SR SL

EP

GR

BF

D

BF

MI

AM

AM

AM

MI

MI

Vertical Tunnel
down to Blue
Door (level 1)

SL

AM

MI

Mine 3—Red Key Area

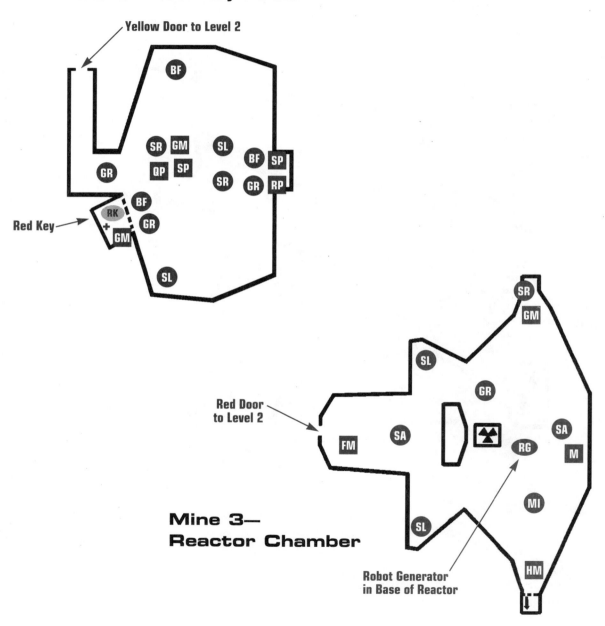

Yellow Door to Level 2

BF

SR GM
QP SP
SL
BF SP
SR GR RP

GR

Red Key

RK BF
GR
GM

SL

SR
GM

SL

GR

Red Door
to Level 2

FM SA

SA
M

RG

MI

SL

Mine 3—
Reactor Chamber

HM

Robot Generator
in Base of Reactor

Mine 4—Robby Station

The starting point for this mine is relatively safe and devoid of any immediate threats. Opening the first door, however, reveals a Centurion behind a force-field who immediately begins lobbing homing missiles at your ship. The best way to deal with him is to use the opening in the floor to drop down for cover, and then pop up and fire after each missile volley until the Centurion is destroyed. As you proceed along level one be very careful not to trip over any mines or linger in front of force-fields with robots on the other side.

When you reach the first door leading to the drop points to level two you will encounter two robot generators, one on each side of the door. These generators are triggered by opening this door. It is best to use this to your advantage by opening the door briefly every few moments to allow the generators to burn themselves out. Once they have done so, the robots stuffed into the chamber on the other side can be picked off one by one.

There is a robot generator hidden in the ceiling above you as you descend to the blue key area. As you make your dash to the blue key, this generator is triggered and starts spewing out Grizzlies. Rush to the key using afterburners, then race back to the opening to level two. You may have to destroy one of the Grizzlies, but this is a better alternative than trying to take on several at once in such little space.

There is standard resistance as you travel through level three to the drop point for level four. On level four there are two robot generators on either side of the energy center. If you are not in need of energy, bypass this area using afterburners on your way to the End Boss. If you desperately need energy, switch to a non-energy weapon and pick each robot off until the generators stop spawning them.

The End Boss area harbors a Boss that teleports and fires a steady stream of homing missiles. The best way to deal with him is to use 'hit-and-fade' tactics—essentially, fly into the main chamber launching everything you've got, then return to the tunnel where you started. This method takes patience but is the most effective for way for dealing with teleporting Bosses. Once the Boss has been destroyed, the exit will trigger and you can leave the mine.

Mine 4—
Level 1

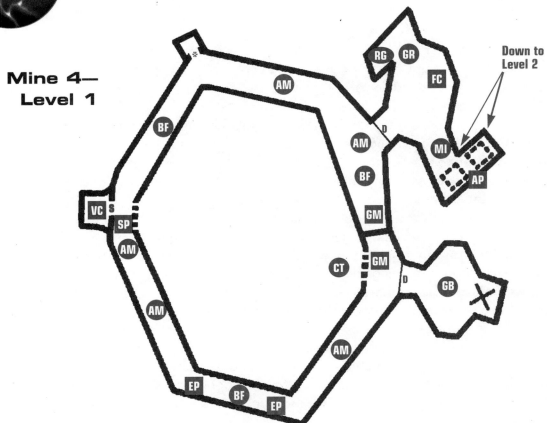

Down to
Level 2

Mine 4—
Blue Key Area

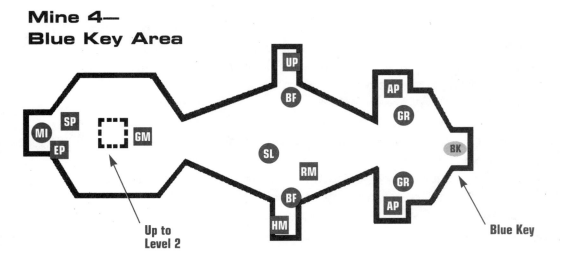

Up to
Level 2

Blue Key

Mine 4—Level 2

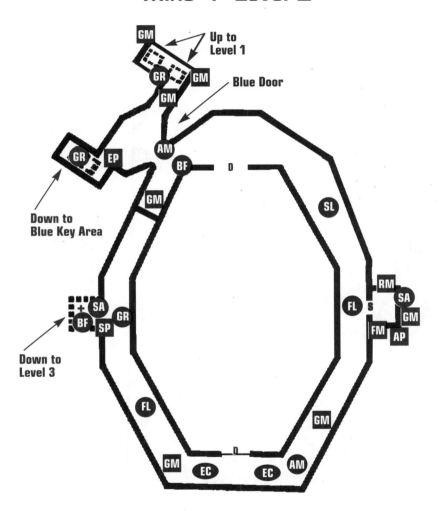

Mine 4—Level 3

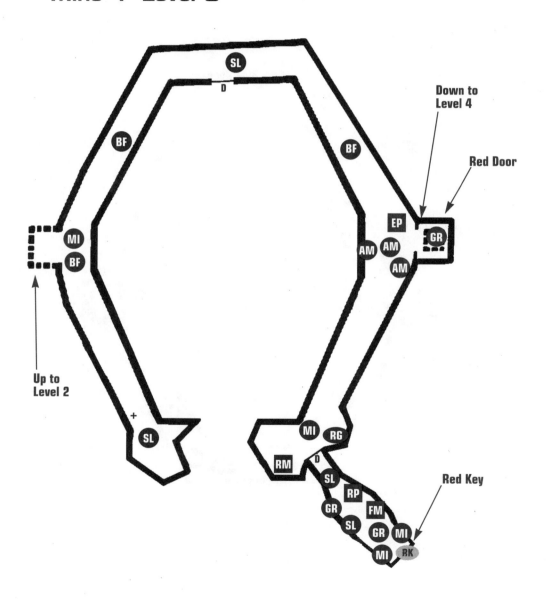

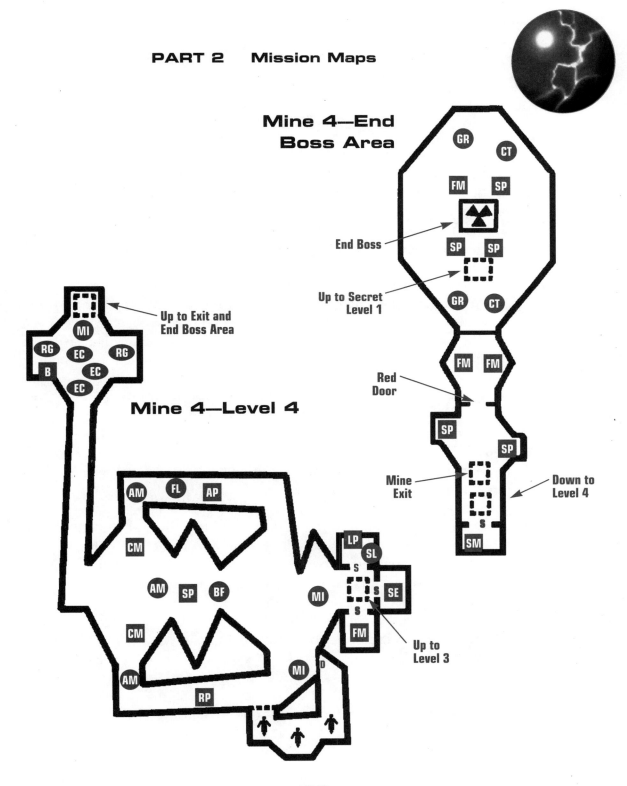

Mine 4—End Boss Area

End Boss

Up to Secret Level 1

Red Door

Mine Exit

Down to Level 4

Up to Exit and End Boss Area

Mine 4—Level 4

Up to Level 3

Mine 5—Seaspring Gorge

Following the destruction of the Robby Mine, you will warp to System 2: Quartzon to take out the Seaspring Gorge mine. In this mine are two new robots: the Triton and the Blue Crab, both of which are extremely fast and carry heavy weaponry.

Exit the entry chamber and fly into the large room. If you want to rescue the Guidebot from its prison, look down into the first chasm you see and fire at its cage set into the wall. Otherwise, pass over the first chasm and go to the second chasm on the opposite side of the room. Go down it.

At the bottom of the chasm is a chamber filled with water and a robot generator set into one of the walls. Once you reach the bottom of the chasm, take the large water corridor that leads *upward*. At the top of the corridor, the corridor branches. Bear right and take the first hole straight down.

At the bottom of the hole, follow the wall around to the right until you reach the chamber with the blue key. Grab it.

Retrieving the blue key seals almost all the holes to the chamber above. Fly to the other side of the grate where you grabbed the blue key. Orient yourself so the grate is behind you, then enter the center corridor (the only corridor that has a floor of water). In the ceiling of this corridor is a hole leading up. Fly up it.

Once up the hole, face the corridor with the panel at the end. Shoot the panel to open the walls sealing you in. Follow the corridor around to the right or left until you come back to the large water corridor flowing down. Fly down it until you are back at the chasm with the robot generator.

Take the other water passage that exits the room leading down. Fly down it until you *almost* reach the bottom, then turn and face the waterfall. You will see there is a passage behind the waterfall (it is directly opposite the "Weapons Testing Area" sign in the room at the bottom of the waterfall). Fly through this hidden passage, and you will find yourself in a water trench. Fly straight down this trench all the way to the opposite wall and turn right to face a shaft upwards. Fly up it.

At the top of the hole you will be in a room with two blue doors. Ignore the blue door right in front of the shaft; take the other one to your right behind the shaft. Follow the corridor around to the right until you reach a room with a high ceiling (if you reach the other blue door first, you've gone too far). At the top of the room is a corridor that leads to the red key. Grab it.

Backtrack through the rooms that led to the red key following the corridor back around to the left. You will find that grabbing the red key has caused grates to seal off the exit. Shoot the panel on the wall to the left of the grate to open the wall and escape back out the blue door you entered from. Once back in the room with the two blue doors, go down the shaft. At the bottom of the shaft, head for the alcove directly opposite the shaft and look for the red door.

Open the red door and enter the room beyond. Fly down the corridor on the opposite side of the room. This leads to the reactor chamber. The reactor is guarded by a force field. First, fire at the panel to the left of the reactor to open walls surrounding the reactor chamber. Then fly a short way through any of the corridors at the bottom of the reactor chamber and you will hear a hum as the force field cuts off. Return to the main reactor chamber and let your weapons chew up the reactor till it explodes.

When the reactor is destroyed, make for the exit. You've got a ways to go, so make it quick. Leave the reactor room via the red door (the corridor that leads to the red door is the only corridor that is on the same level as the reactor platform in the room). Go out the red door and follow the wall around to the right until you find yourself in a water trench. When you reach an intersection of trenches, take the first water trench to your right (it will have a sign "Warning: Low Gravity" above it), then continue to follow the wall around to your right. You will eventually find yourself in a *huge* chasm room . . . fly past this room and take the next passage up. This rocky passage leads to a room that contains the exit.

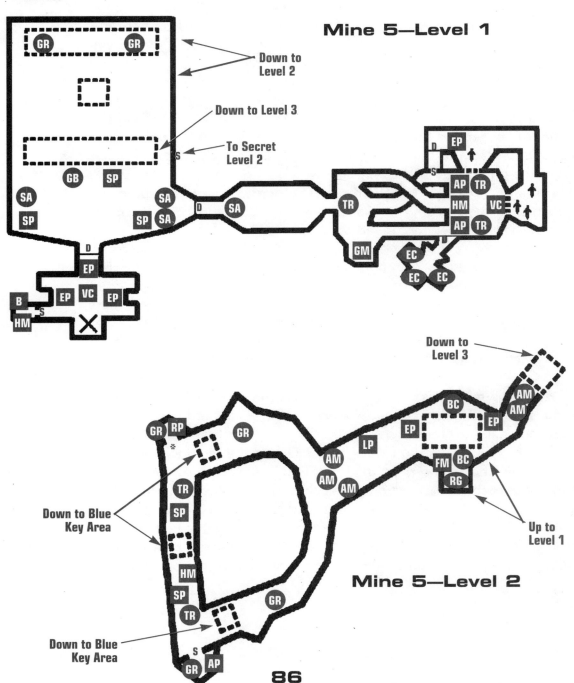

Mine 5—Level 1

Down to Level 2

Down to Level 3

To Secret Level 2

Down to Level 3

Up to Level 1

Down to Blue Key Area

Down to Blue Key Area

Mine 5—Level 2

Mine 5—Level 3

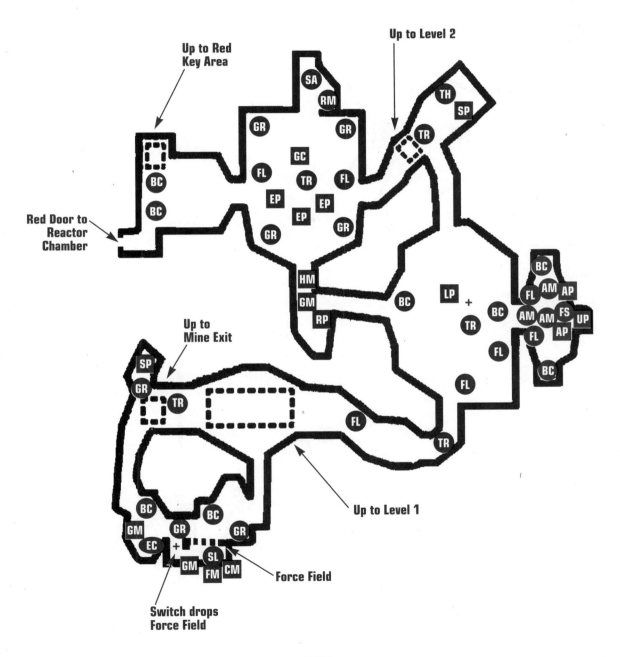

Up to Level 2

Up to Red
Key Area

Red Door to
Reactor
Chamber

Up to
Mine Exit

Up to Level 1

Force Field

Switch drops
Force Field

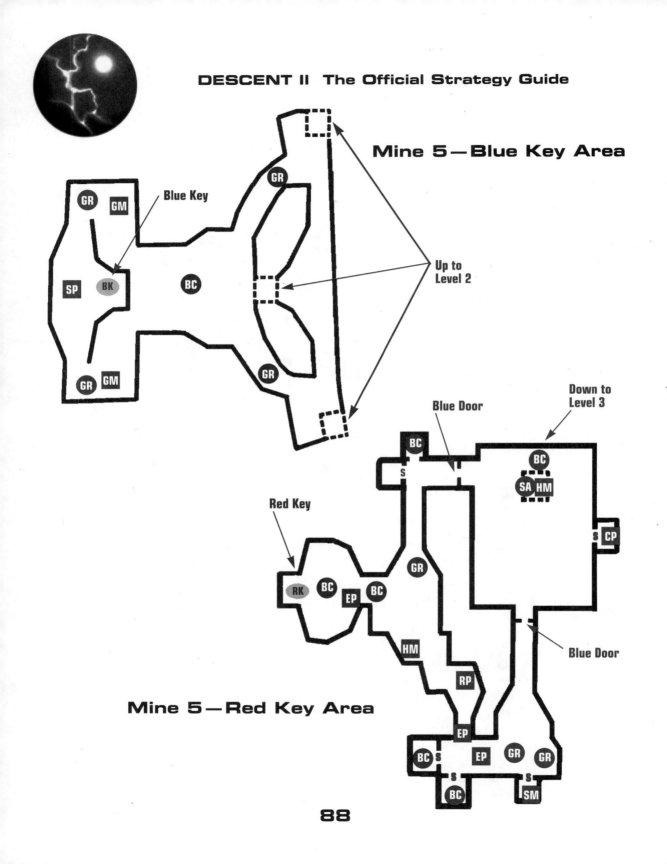

Mine 5—Blue Key Area

Blue Key

Up to
Level 2

Mine 5—Red Key Area

Red Key

Blue Door

Down to
Level 3

Blue Door

Mine 5 — Reactor Chamber

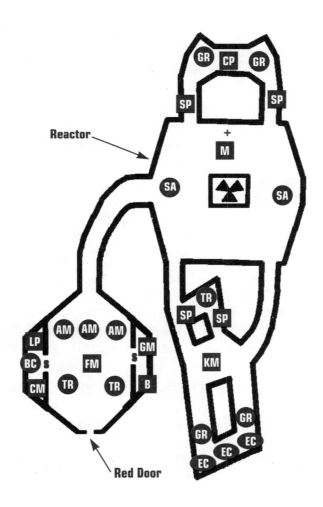

Reactor

Red Door

Mine 6—The Well

To your left lies the Guidebot trapped in its cage. Free it if you feel it's necessary.

The only exit from this room is the well directly opposite your starting point. Fly down it and through the door at the bottom. Past the door is a room. On the opposite wall (indicated by green walls) is another well that leads down. Take it. At the bottom of the well are two branching passages; take the passage that heads upstream and when the ceiling starts to rise, nose your craft upward to get the blue key.

In the same room as the blue key, there is a blue door. Open it and head down the shaft. At the bottom of the shaft is a corridor that leads into a room with the yellow key. The key is behind the block in the middle of the room, so fly around the block and snag the key.

Once you have the yellow key, a grate will seal off the exit to this room. Shoot the panel that lies behind the yellow key and another exit will open on one of the walls to the right of the key. Take this passage downstream. You will pass through a waterfall and into a water trench flanked by two signs proclaiming this as a "Weapon Testing Area." When you reach this area, head straight up and snag the red key at the room at the top of the shaft. (Note that this room also contains the exit.)

Fly back down the shaft to the area flanked by the "Weapon Testing Area" signs. Fly down the water trench to the cross intersection and hang a right. Within a second, you'll see the red door. Open it, enter the room, and let the reactor have it with a little plasma cannon tenderness.

Exit the room via the red door, fly straight ahead through the water trench, and take the first left back toward the area flanked by the "Weapon Testing Area" signs. Once there, head back up the shaft where you got the red key and take the exit and you're outta there.

Mine 6—Level 1a

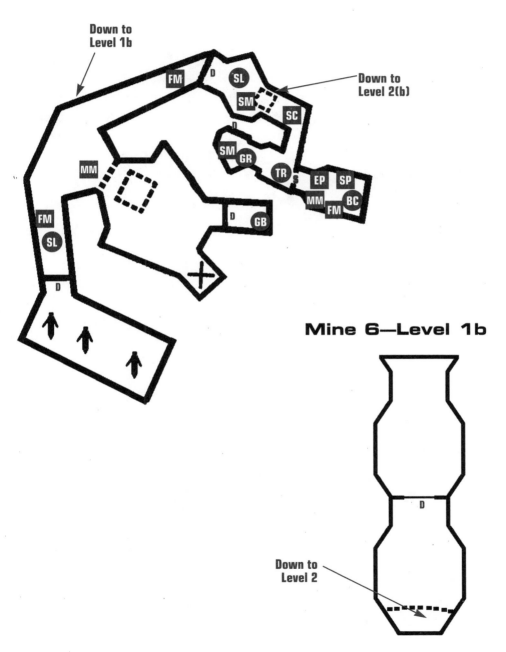

Mine 6—Level 1b

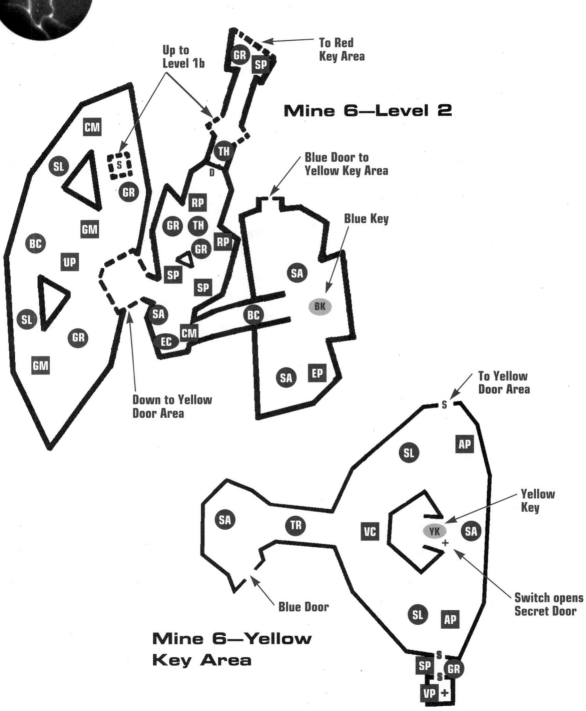

Up to
Level 1b

To Red
Key Area

Mine 6—Level 2

Blue Door to
Yellow Key Area

Blue Key

Down to Yellow
Door Area

To Yellow
Door Area

Yellow
Key

Switch opens
Secret Door

Blue Door

Mine 6—Yellow
Key Area

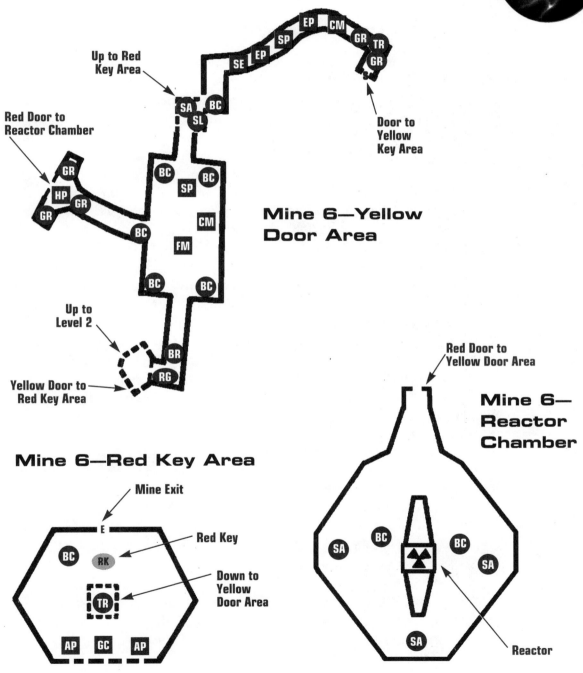

Up to Red
Key Area

Red Door to
Reactor Chamber

Door to
Yellow
Key Area

GR

HP GR

GR

BC

SP

BC

CM

FM

BC

BC

SA
SL

BC

Mine 6—Yellow
Door Area

SE EP SP EP CM GR TR

GR

Up to
Level 2

Yellow Door to
Red Key Area

BR

RG

Red Door to
Yellow Door Area

Mine 6—
Reactor
Chamber

Mine 6—Red Key Area

Mine Exit

E

Red Key

BC RK

Down to
Yellow
Door Area

TR

AP GC AP

To Level 2

SA BC BC SA

SA

Reactor

Mine 7—Coralbank Quarry

Coralbank Quarry will be the first time War Helm robots appear in the game. They can fire multiple Mercury missiles at you, so be cautious and try to shoot them down before they can draw a bead on you.

You start in a cross-shaped chamber with one exit (a corridor) directly in front of you. In the floor in front of you is the Guidebot trapped in its cage.

The only exit from this room is the corridor directly in front of you. Fly down it and through the door. Bear left and hug the right wall, passing the large metal pillar on your left and flying up the waterfall.

At the top of the waterfall, you'll enter a room with a corridor to the right. Take it, then take the first corridor to the left. *Keep bearing to the left and down* and you will come to a room at the bottom of a waterfall that has water running through the center and metal floors sloping up flanking it. On the room opposite the entrance is a metal grillwork shaft leading down. Take it.

A few more dips down after the grillwork shaft, you will come to a fork. Take the right branch. Hug the right wall as you pass through two rooms and grab the blue key where it floats in its alcove.

After snagging the blue key, you will have to backtrack almost all the way to your starting place. To do this, leave the way you came into the room with the blue key and hug the left wall until you reach the grillwork shaft. Go up the shaft, straight through the room with the sloping metal floors that flank the exits then head up, *bearing to the right and up* until you come the green room whose only other exit is a corridor to the left that has black and yellow construction hatching at its entrance. Take this corridor and head down the waterfall until you reach the chasm-like room with the large metal pillar you passed. Once you hit the large metal pillar, bank right and down the waterfall.

You might be tempted to follow the waterfall all the way down to the bottom. Don't. Instead hug the ceiling and look for the first shaft up. You'll enter a room with an energy center and a blue door at the top of the room. Open the door, then hug the left wall (you'll pass a robot generator) and then head down.

Going down the shaft, you'll be following the path of a waterfall and heading down a grillwork shaft. Keep descending until the waterfall levels out. At this point, there will be a grillwork door through which the water flows into a large green room. Open the door, enter the green room, and take the exit the water flows out of. From this point on, *stay low and hug the right wall.* You'll wind through several tall narrow caverns until you come to a room with the yellow key directly in front of you. Grab it.

No need to backtrack here. In the room with the yellow key, there is a shaft in the ceiling. Take it up till it levels out, then hug the wall to the left until you hit a yellow door. Open it and follow the corridor until it hits a robot generator set into the ceiling. Turn left and pass through the waterfall you see there. Follow the waterfall down into the room below and exit through the door on the opposite side of the room (ignore the cage and the robots in it). Keep following the corridor past the door. You will pass through two waterfalls. After the second waterfall, look for a shaft up as the corridor turns to the left. Take the shaft up to a well-lighted room, level off and take the only exit out of the room. The passage will pass a robot generator hidden by a waterfall. When you see the generator, bear to the left. You will almost immediately come to a door. Open it and head down the shaft to the bottom of the waterfall.

At the bottom, you will see a glowing red light behind one of the waterfalls which leads to the red key. Fly through the waterfall and snag the key.

In the same area as the key shoot the panels on either side to open walls in the Quarry and allow you to quickly exit the area. Leave the area where you got the key by flying halfway up the shaft into the first room of water you encounter. Head up the other waterfall in the room, passing through a waterfall that has a robot generator on the other side, visible through the waterfall. Once you pass through the waterfall, head straight past the robot generator. Continue straight down the corridor and pass through a yellow access grate.

You will find yourself at the bottom of a huge waterfall. Keep heading up the waterfall, hugging the water (*not* the ceiling) until you emerge

Mine 7—Level 1

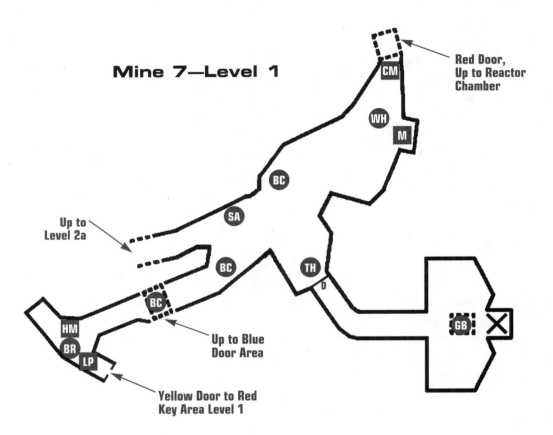

Red Door,
Up to Reactor
Chamber

Up to
Level 2a

Up to Blue
Door Area

Yellow Door to Red
Key Area Level 1

PART 2   Mission Maps

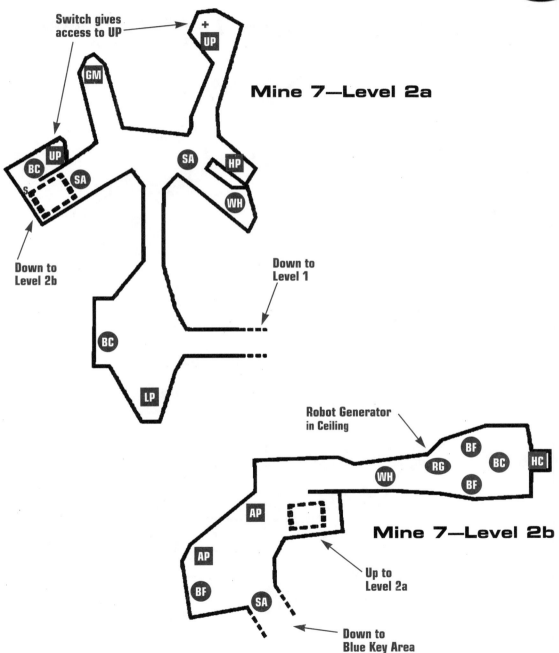

Switch gives access to UP

Mine 7—Level 2a

Down to Level 2b

Down to Level 1

Robot Generator in Ceiling

Mine 7—Level 2b

Up to Level 2a

Down to Blue Key Area

97

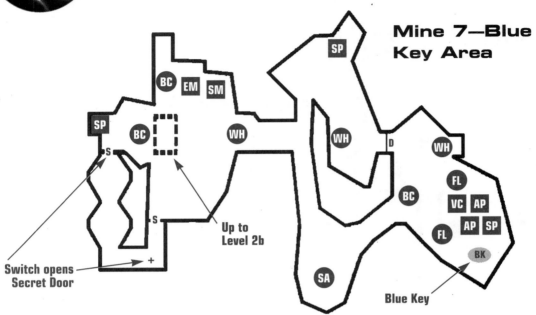

Mine 7—Blue Key Area

SP

BC EM SM

SP

BC

WH

WH

D

WH

S

BC

FL

VC AP

AP SP

S

FL

BK

Up to
Level 2b

SA

Blue Key

Switch opens
Secret Door

+

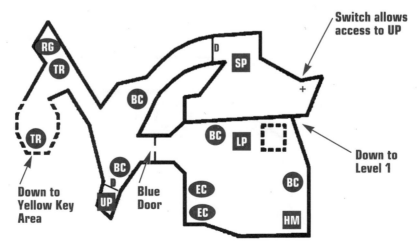

Mine 7—Blue Door Area

Switch allows
access to UP

RG

TR

D

SP

BC

+

TR

BC LP

Down to
Level 1

BC

BC

D

EC

UP

EC

BC

Down to
Yellow Key
Area

Blue
Door

HM

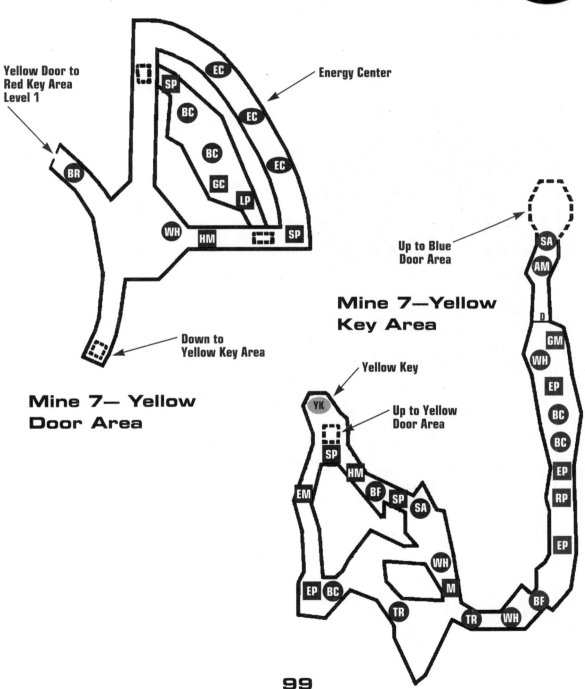

Yellow Door to
Red Key Area
Level 1

Energy Center

**Mine 7—Yellow
Key Area**

Up to Blue
Door Area

Yellow Key

Up to Yellow
Door Area

Down to
Yellow Key Area

**Mine 7— Yellow
Door Area**

99

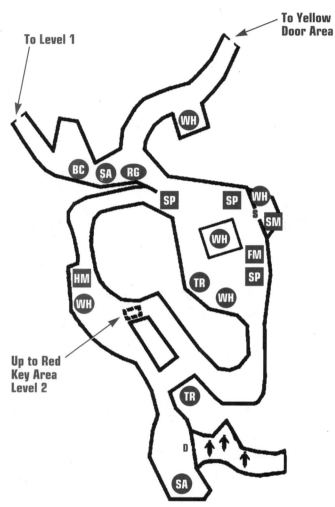

To Yellow
Door Area

To Level 1

WH

BC SA RG

SP SP WH

SM

WH

FM

HM SP

WH TR

WH

Up to Red
Key Area
Level 2

TR

D

SA

Mine 7—Red Key
Area Level 1

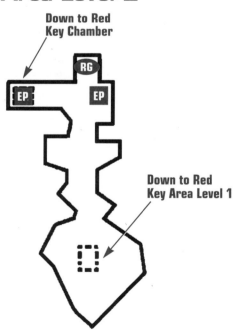

Mine 7—Red Key
Area Level 2

**Down to Red
Key Chamber**

RG

EP EP

**Down to Red
Key Area Level 1**

Mine 7—Red Key Chamber

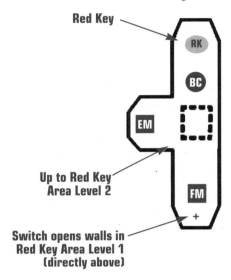

Red Key

RK

BC

EM

Up to Red Key
Area Level 2

FM

+

Switch opens walls in
Red Key Area Level 1
(directly above)

Mine 7—Reactor Area

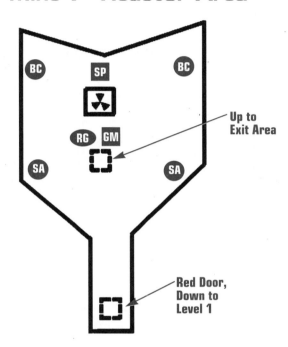

BC   SP   BC

RG GM

SA   SA

Up to
Exit Area

Red Door,
Down to
Level 1

Mine 7—Exit Area

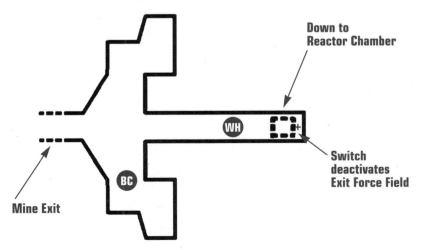

Down to
Reactor Chamber

WH   +

Switch
deactivates
Exit Force Field

BC

Mine Exit

back at the huge metal pillar room you passed through twice before. Keep heading through the water chasm. You will pass a robot generator on the right (camouflaged by a waterfall) and then the chasm dead-ends into a shaft up (the shaft is another waterfall). Take the waterfall up to the red access door.

Past the red access door, you will find yourself in a caged room with one exit door. Open the door, pass through the waterfall beyond into the main reactor room and blow the hell out of the reactor.

After destroying the reactor, look for a shaft up in the ceiling of the reactor room (it should be right above the entrance to the room). Fly through the shaft for a short distance, then do a full reverse and fly back toward the reactor room. Look for a panel directly in front of you. Shoot it to deactivate the force field in front of the exit. Then turn around and resume your exit. You'll pass through one more waterfall and dip down into a small room. You will then be able to make a clean get away through the exit.

Mine 8—The Riverbed Mine

In the room just beneath your starting position is the cage of your poor, lonely Guidebot. Fly into the chamber before you right over to the "Danger: Radiation" sign, then turn around. The Guidebot cage will be right in front of you.

Acquiring the blue key is pretty easy. Bear right from your starting position and dip down to the first door you see. Open it, and the blue key rests in the middle of the chamber beyond. Destroy all robots in the room that dare oppose your plasma-pounding onslaught.

Okay, you've got the blue key. Now there is only one other door in the room—it's on the wall left of the entrance. Shoot the panel to the left of the door to unlock it, then go through the door and take the shaft down to the water level. (Watch out—there is a robot generator at the bottom.) After securing the area, open the blue door at the bottom of the shaft, but be careful before entering the room beyond: There is another robot generator on the ceiling guarding a shaft upwards. Head up the shaft to the first leveling off area and scan the area for the yellow key. It is stored behind a grate. Navigate around the grate area and pick up the yellow key.

Exit down the shaft you entered to get to the yellow key room, past the robot generator and into the room beyond. Look for another blue door (though not the one you initially used to enter this room). It will be on the opposite side of the room as the other blue door. Once you pass through the robot generator, go to the bottom of the room and look up. You will see a shaft up and to the side of the robot generator on the ceiling. Take it and follow it down and to the right to find the second blue door.

Past that door, go down into the trench. Make a left (away from the energy converters, but back up and recharge for a while if you need to) and then proceed down the trench. You will see a yellow door on your right. Open it and descend down the shaft.

At the bottom of the shaft is a red access door and another corridor. Fly down the corridor, hugging the left wall. You'll enter a large room, but keep hugging the left wall until you see an alcove set into it with the red and black hatching that shows where the red key is placed. Enter the bottom of the alcove and snag the red key.

Backtrack to the shaft with the red access door (hugging the right wall to get there after leaving the red key alcove) and open it.

From here, make sure you have grabbed all weapon and shield power-ups that you can. The reactor is ugly, mobile, and packing a lot of firepower. Here is where you will encounter the Mine Boss behind the invasion of the Quartzon system. He's not especially tough (use hit and run tactics), but he is surrounded by a number of heavy robots and smart mine dropping mechanoids that can wear down your defenses.

After defeating the Boss, return to the first level of the Boss's stronghold around the red access door and look for one of two shafts up. You can choose to leave through the central corridor and leave the Riverbed mine behind you, or take a passage (the one directly opposite of the hostages) and head upwards to a hole in the roof. This will take you to Secret Level Zeta Aquilae-2: The Hurdle Chase.

Mine 8—Level 1

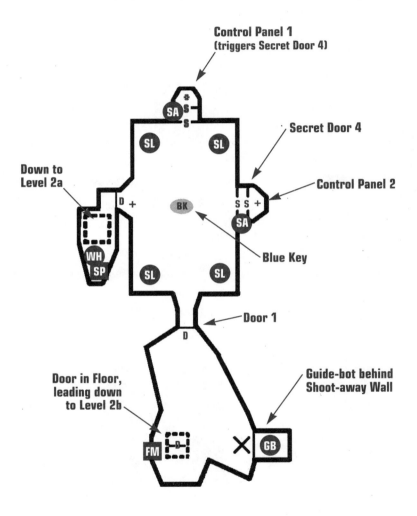

Control Panel 1
(triggers Secret Door 4)

Secret Door 4

Control Panel 2

Down to
Level 2a

Blue Key

Door 1

Door in Floor,
leading down
to Level 2b

Guide-bot behind
Shoot-away Wall

Mine 8—Level 2

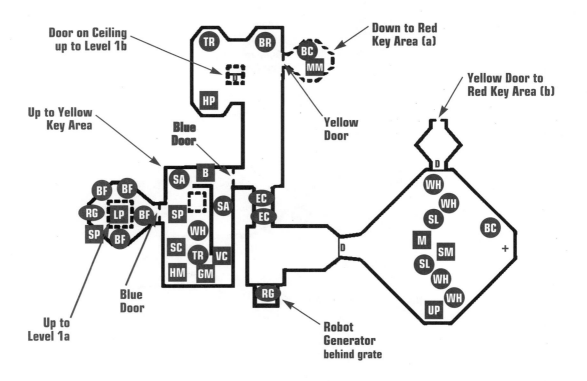

Door on Ceiling
up to Level 1b

Down to Red
Key Area (a)

Yellow Door to
Red Key Area (b)

Up to Yellow
Key Area

Blue
Door

Yellow
Door

Up to
Level 1a

Blue
Door

Robot
Generator
behind grate

Mine 8—Red Key Area

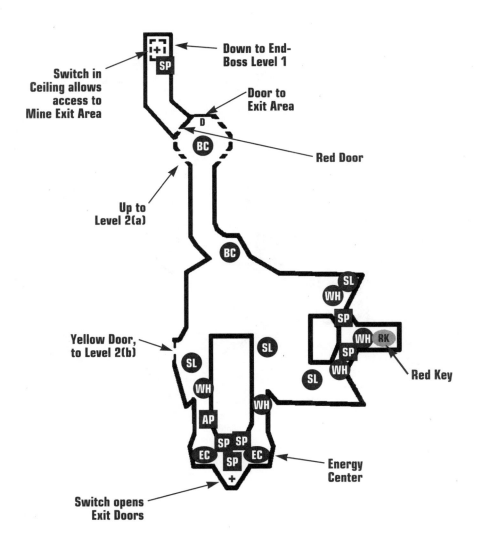

Down to End-Boss Level 1

Switch in Ceiling allows access to Mine Exit Area

Door to Exit Area

Red Door

Up to Level 2(a)

Yellow Door, to Level 2(b)

Red Key

Energy Center

Switch opens Exit Doors

Mine 8—End-Boss
Level 1

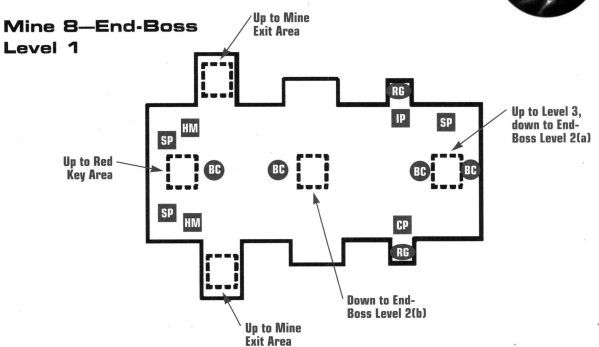

Up to Mine
Exit Area

RG

IP   SP

Up to Level 3,
down to End-
Boss Level 2(a)

HM

SP

Up to Red
Key Area

BC   BC   BC   BC

SP
HM

CP

RG

Down to End-
Boss Level 2(b)

Up to Mine
Exit Area

Mine 8—End-Boss
Level 2

Down to End-
Boss Level 1(a)

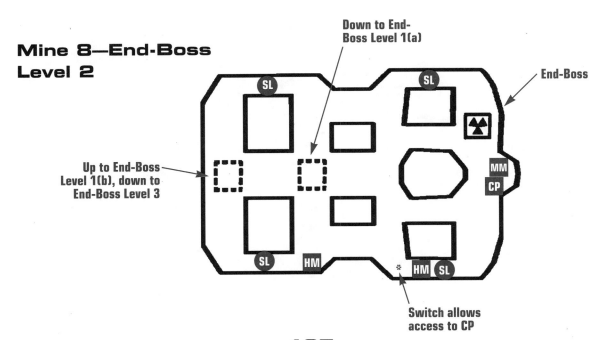

End-Boss

SL   SL

Up to End-Boss
Level 1(b), down to
End-Boss Level 3

MM
CP

SL   HM

HM   SL

Switch allows
access to CP

107

Mine 8—End-Boss Level 3

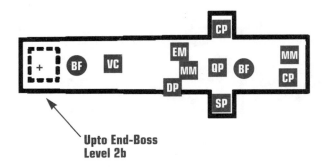

Upto End-Boss
Level 2b

Mine 8—Exit Area

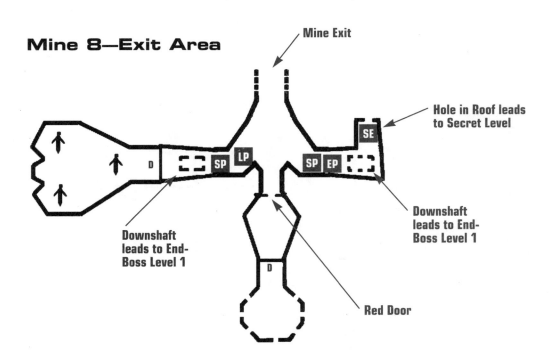

Mine Exit

Hole in Roof leads
to Secret Level

Downshaft
leads to End-
Boss Level 1

Downshaft
leads to End-
Boss Level 1

Red Door

Mine 9—Firewalker Mine

As soon as you appear in this level fire a flare at the far wall. Shoot the control panel behind the secret door. This deactivates the force field behind the lava falls. Travel through the lava fall and follow the passage all the way down until it ends at the red door. From there, make a right turn and travel to the end of the tunnel where the blue key is located.

If you want to free the Guidebot, return to the insertion point, exit the door and follow the right wall. When you reach another door, stop! Turn your ship around and go back the way you came. You will come across a door you passed over, but didn't see. Destroy the door to release the Guidebot.

To get to the yellow key, retrace your steps to the insertion point. Exit through the only door in that area. Proceed in a straight line from the door until the floor drops down into a lava pit. Go down the lava pit, and on the left hand side there will be a passage. Go up the passage and turn right. This should lead you to the blue door. Once through the blue door, turn left, go through the door and follow the passage until you come to a control panel with a grate placed in the ceiling right above it. Right underneath the grate there is a tunnel going down. At the bottom of the tunnel there will be a room with another tunnel leading down. Take it. You should now be in a room with three lava falls flowing down the sides of a passage leading up. At the top of this passage you will find the yellow key. Once you get the yellow key a secret door opens at the base of the tunnel, so watch out!

As you go back out the blue door, turn left and the yellow door will be on the left hand side. The first room through the yellow door is essentially an oval room with two passages on the opposite side. Fly to either one of the passages and when you enter the room there will be a pit between the two passages. If you go down the pit, it will lead you to the red key.

Retrace your steps and proceed back to the insertion point. From the insertion point, travel down the passage behind lava falls. At the end of this passage will be the red door. Beyond the red door, at the very back of this area will be the reactor. You know what to do here.

Mine 9—Level 1

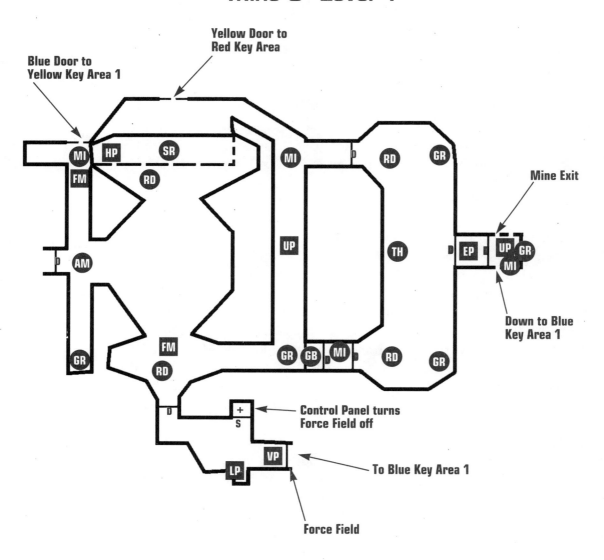

Yellow Door to
Red Key Area

Blue Door to
Yellow Key Area 1

Mine Exit

Down to Blue
Key Area 1

Control Panel turns
Force Field off

To Blue Key Area 1

Force Field

Mine 9—
Blue Key Area

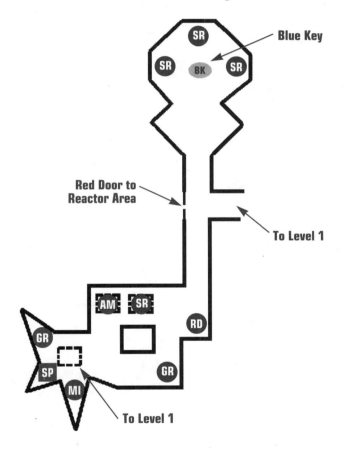

Blue Key

Red Door to
Reactor Area

To Level 1

To Level 1

Mine 9—Yellow Key Area Level 1

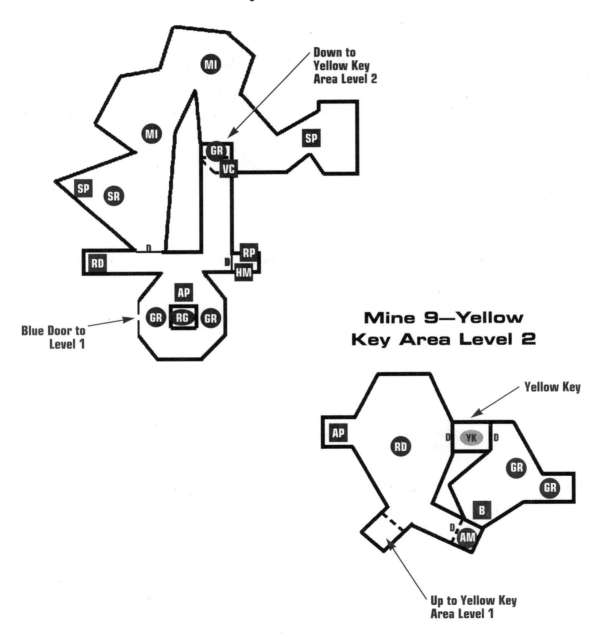

Down to
Yellow Key
Area Level 2

Blue Door to
Level 1

Mine 9—Yellow
Key Area Level 2

Yellow Key

Up to Yellow Key
Area Level 1

Mine 9—Red Key Area Level 1

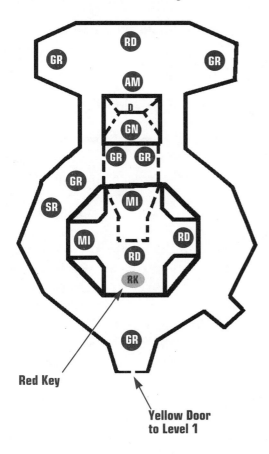

Red Key

Yellow Door
to Level 1

Mine 9—Reactor Area

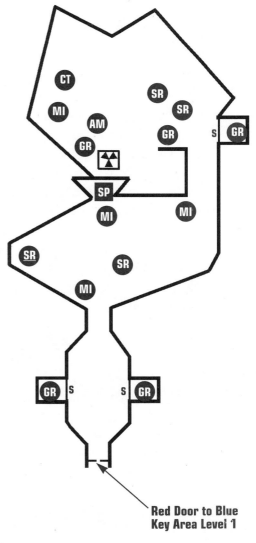

Red Door to Blue
Key Area Level 1

As you exit the red door, make a right. Follow the left side of the tunnel, always taking the left passage. When you notice a mesh type grating along the left wall, scan the ceiling and there should be a tunnel leading up with the exit at the end of it.

Mine 10—Lavafalls Extraction Center

From the insertion point, travel all the way to the end of the hallway and turn right. A short way down the passage you'll hear and see your Guidebot friend firing flares from his prison in the ceiling. Destroy the door to let the Guidebot out.

Returning to the insertion point, travel to the end of the hallway and turn left. When you pass through the door you'll be in a medium sized room with lava at the bottom. At the bottom of the room there is a passage that will take you through to two grate-type tunnels. Be prepared for a massive onslaught from enemy robots as you pass through. Eventually you'll fly into a large room with lava and a bridge running across it. Make a left as you enter. If you look at the lava, you'll notice that it's flowing into a hole in the floor. Fly down the hole and pull up quick, unless you want to slam into a molten bed of lava. The blue key will be in plain sight.

After retrieving the blue key, go back up the lava hole and stop. If you look carefully at the lava flowing from the upper cavern area to the lower cavern area, you'll be able to see a passage behind the lava fall. Follow this passage to the blue door. Once past the blue door, be sure to destroy all Kamikaze robots. One of them is carrying the yellow key.

Keep flying down that same tunnel until you reach a giant lava flow falling from the ceiling. Travel in and up the lava flow. Flying through this next area, you pass under a grate tunnel and through a door where you encounter a second blue door. Straight through the blue door is the yellow door. Follow the passage beyond the yellow door and just past the second door you'll have a choice to turn right or go up into the ceiling. Take the right passage all the way to the end. There will be a one way door with a Kamikaze on the other side who is carrying the red key. If you

PART 2   Mission Maps

Mine 10—Level 1

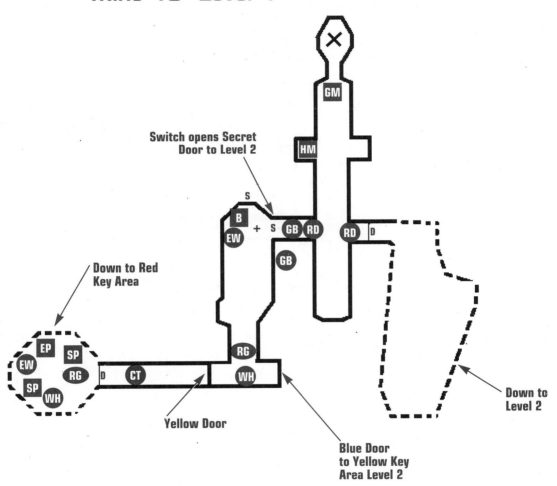

115

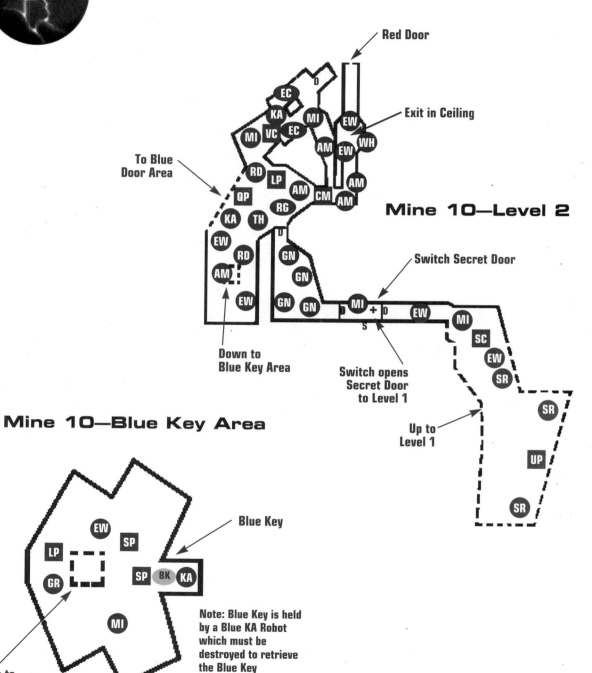

Red Door

Exit in Ceiling

To Blue
Door Area

Mine 10—Level 2

Switch Secret Door

Down to
Blue Key Area

Switch opens
Secret Door
to Level 1

Up to
Level 1

Mine 10—Blue Key Area

Blue Key

Note: Blue Key is held
by a Blue KA Robot
which must be
destroyed to retrieve
the Blue Key

Up to
Level 2

116

Mine 10—Blue Door Area

Mine 10—Yellow Key Area Level 1

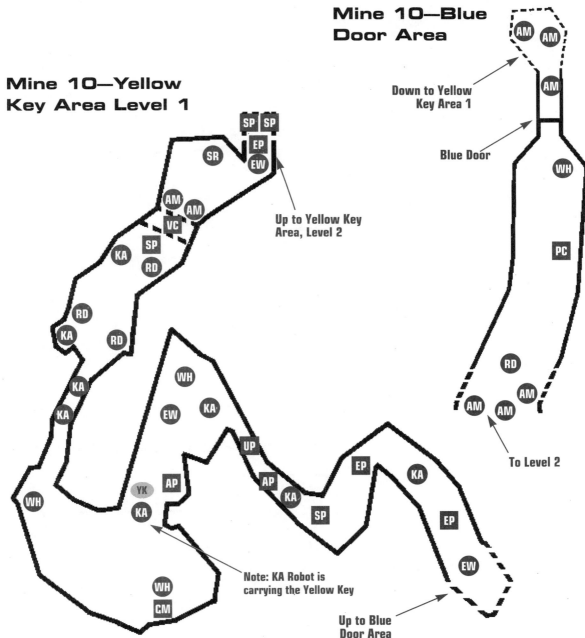

Down to Yellow Key Area 1

Blue Door

Up to Yellow Key Area, Level 2

To Level 2

Note: KA Robot is carrying the Yellow Key

Up to Blue Door Area

117

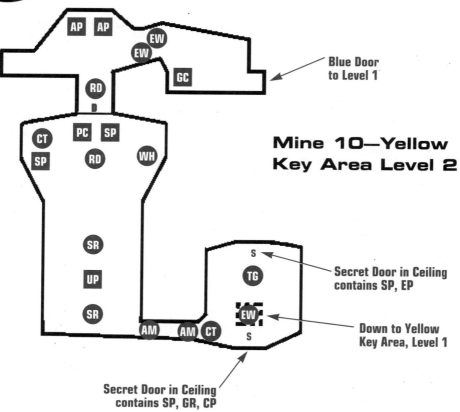

Blue Door
to Level 1

Mine 10—Yellow Key Area Level 2

Secret Door in Ceiling
contains SP, EP

Down to Yellow
Key Area, Level 1

Secret Door in Ceiling
contains SP, GR, CP

Mine 10—Red Key Chamber

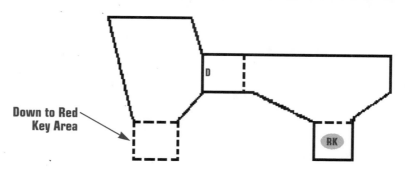

Down to Red
Key Area

Mine 10—Red Key Area

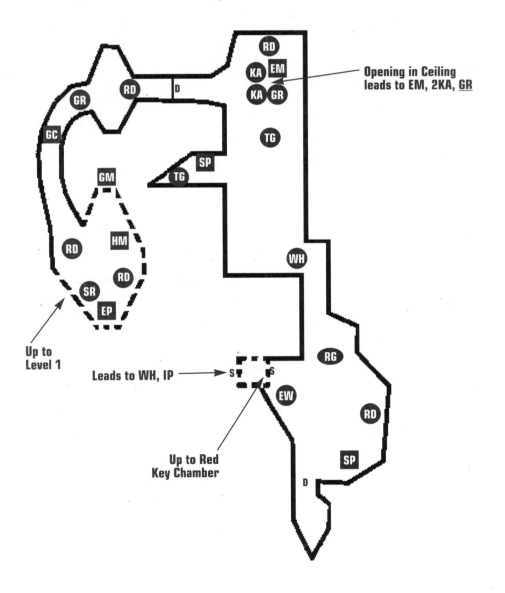

Opening in Ceiling
leads to EM, 2KA, <u>GR</u>

Up to
Level 1

Leads to WH, IP ➞

Up to Red
Key Chamber

Mine 10—Reactor Level 1

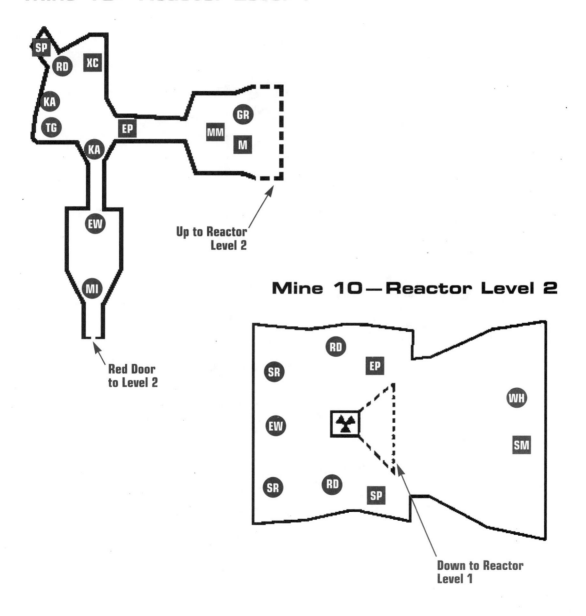

Mine 10—Reactor Level 2

get trapped in that room there is a control panel located in that room that you can use to unlock the door.

Retrace your steps to the yellow door. As you exit the yellow door make a left and go through the next door. This will put you back near the insertion point. Go straight and follow the passage until you reach the large lava room with the bridge running across it. Make a right as you enter the room and follow the passage going down. This will lead you to the red door. Once past the red door, follow the lava down until the passage appears to dead end in a lava fall. Go through the lava fall and head up. The reactor will be in that room.

Once you have destroyed the reactor, go quickly to the red door. Just outside the red door is the mine exit located in the ceiling.

Mine 11—Coalbank Shaft

From insertion point, take the passage down. About half way down the passage, there's a door behind which is the Guidebot.

After rescuing your Guidebot, continue your descent and go through the door at the bottom. Follow the right wall until you encounter a mine shaft leading down. Go down the mine shaft and you'll find an area with pockets of lava, with a door on the far side. Go through the door and follow the right wall. This will lead you all the way to the blue key.

Once you retrieve the blue key and are flying back out of that area, you'll see a pit with lava flowing in it. Go down into the pit and follow the passage to a large red room with a force field tunnel located at the top. On the left side of the room is a door you need to go through. Fly up and to the right to the blue door. (Now might be a good time to save your game.) Once through the blue door, there is another door across the room and a little to the left. Go through the door and down. Take the left passage. To the right, you see the yellow key behind a force field, straight is a lava fall, and to the left is a passage leading to the hostages. Take the left passage and destroy the control panel located right outside the hostage doors. This will deactivate the force field around the yellow key.

Mine 11—Level 1

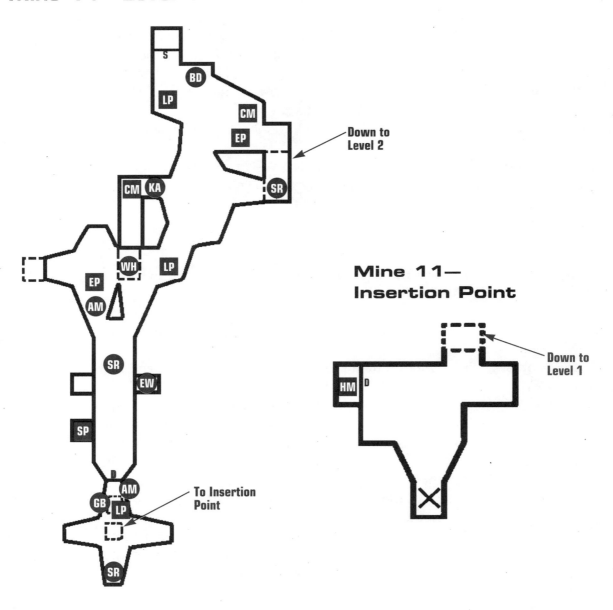

Down to
Level 2

Mine 11—
Insertion Point

Down to
Level 1

To Insertion
Point

Mine 11—Level 2a

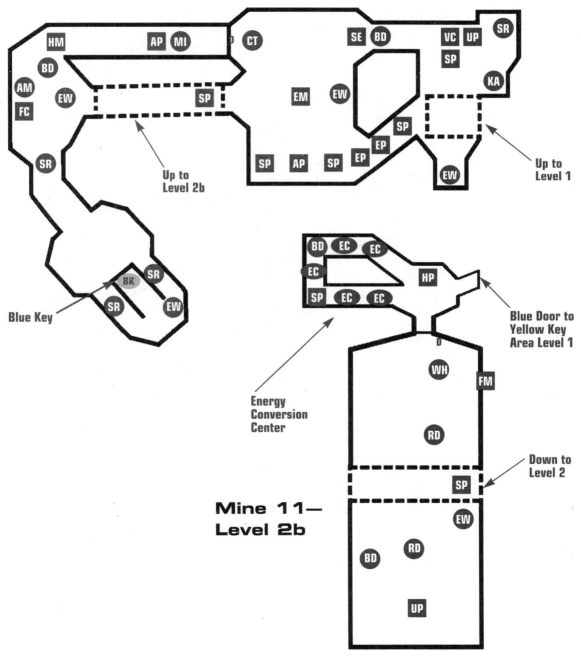

Up to
Level 2b

Blue Key

Up to
Level 1

Energy
Conversion
Center

Blue Door to
Yellow Key
Area Level 1

Down to
Level 2

Mine 11—
Level 2b

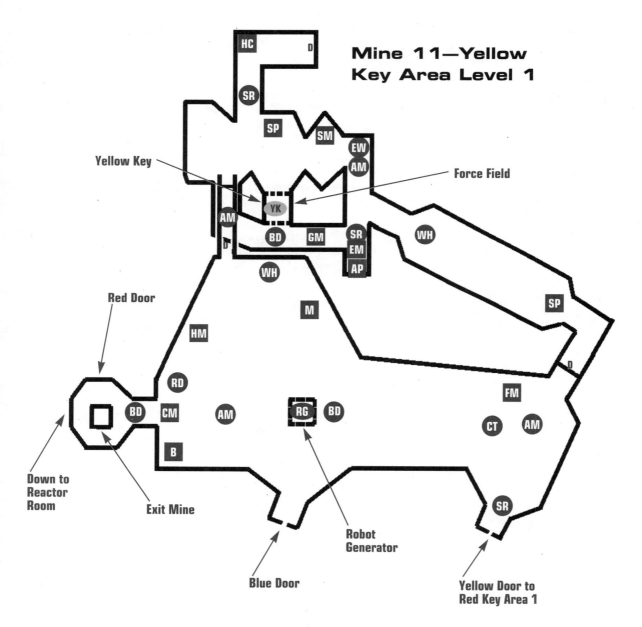

Mine 11—Yellow Key Area Level 1

Yellow Key

Force Field

Red Door

Down to Reactor Room

Exit Mine

Robot Generator

Blue Door

Yellow Door to Red Key Area 1

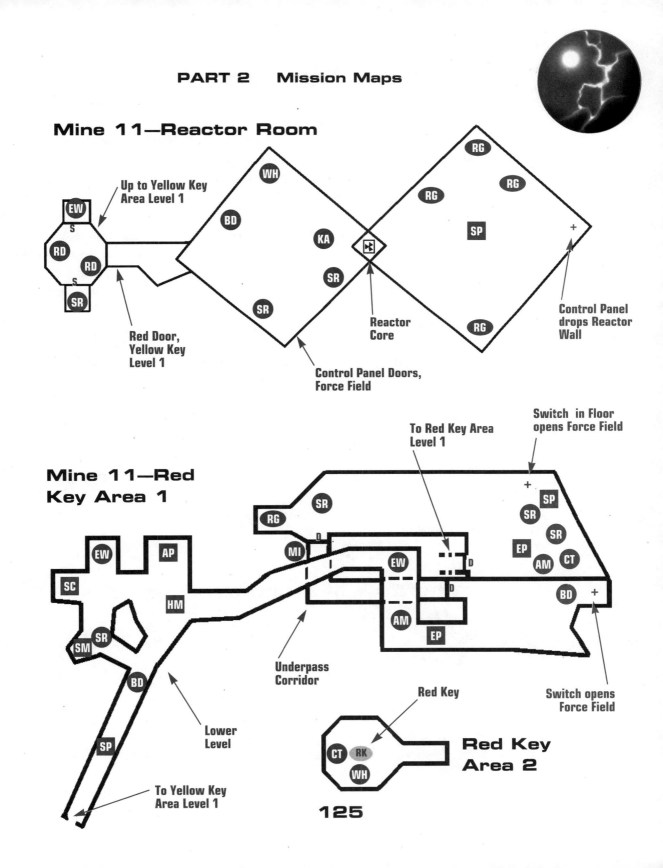

Mine 11—Reactor Room

Up to Yellow Key
Area Level 1

Red Door,
Yellow Key
Level 1

Reactor
Core

Control Panel Doors,
Force Field

Control Panel
drops Reactor
Wall

Switch in Floor
opens Force Field

To Red Key Area
Level 1

Mine 11—Red
Key Area 1

Underpass
Corridor

Lower
Level

To Yellow Key
Area Level 1

Red Key

Switch opens
Force Field

Red Key
Area 2

Return to the blue door. Face the large room with the blue door to the rear of the ship. Follow the right wall until you reach the yellow door. Once through the yellow door and past the force field corridor, follow the left wall until you encounter a passage down. Follow this passage to a room with a force field blocking a passage and a fence blocking off another room with a force field ceiling. Destroy the control panel located in this room to deactivate the force field, then follow the cleared passage to the other side of fence. Destroy the control panel located on the floor to turn the force field off. Go up past the deactivated force field and through the door to the red key.

Return to the yellow door. Turn left after exiting the yellow door. Fly down into second pit area. At the bottom of the area there is a passage that leads to the red door. Fly through the red door then down. At base of the lava fall there is a passage. Fly down through the lava flow. You should now be in a chamber with a force field and grate floor. To deactivate the field, go to the right of the lava fall and shoot the control panel located on the ceiling in that corner. This will reveal a passage to a similar shaped room. In the far corner of the new room, shoot the control panel mounted to the ceiling. This will drop the walls around the reactor. Start shooting—fast.

Retrace your steps to the red door. The exit is located in the ceiling just outside red door.

Mine 12—Magnacore Station

From the insertion point, proceed straight ahead through the door. Go up and over the wall. The Guidebot will be trapped behind the door. Destroy the door to free the Guidebot.

From the Guidebot's cell go right and enter the door. Follow the passage and take the first left. Fly straight through the door and across a large room. This will take you to a lava lined passage at the base of the tunnel. Go straight down the tunnel until you come to the blue key. You must shoot all seven control panels to deactivate the force field. There

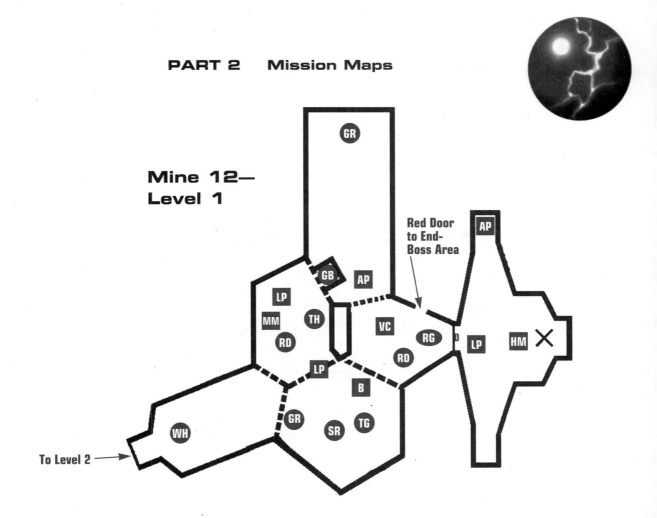

Mine 12— Level 1

Red Door to End- Boss Area

To Level 2

Mine 12—Level 2a

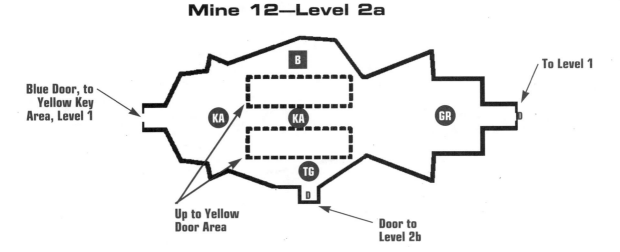

Blue Door, to Yellow Key Area, Level 1

To Level 1

Up to Yellow Door Area

Door to Level 2b

Mine 12—Level 2b

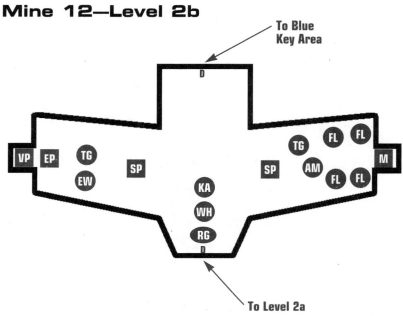

To Blue
Key Area

To Level 2a

Mine 12—Yellow Door Area

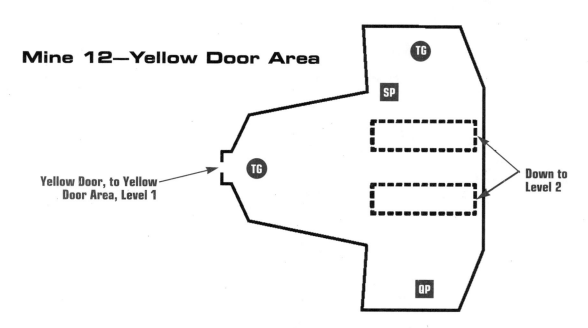

Yellow Door, to Yellow
Door Area, Level 1

Down to
Level 2

Mine 12—Blue Key Area

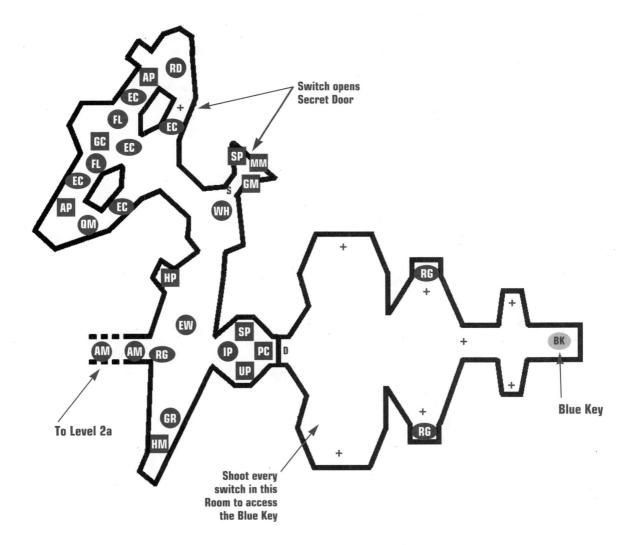

Switch opens
Secret Door

Blue Key

Shoot every
switch in this
Room to access
the Blue Key

To Level 2a

Mine 12—Yellow Key Area Level 1

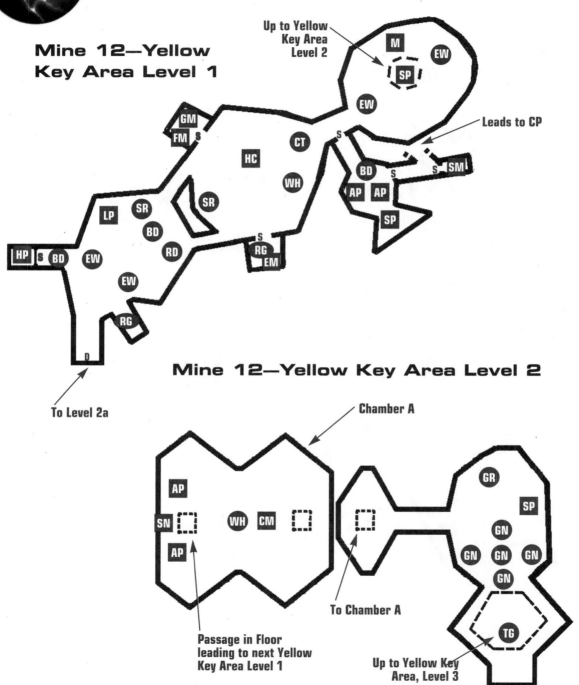

Up to Yellow
Key Area
Level 2

Leads to CP

Mine 12—Yellow Key Area Level 2

To Level 2a

Chamber A

To Chamber A

Passage in Floor
leading to next Yellow
Key Area Level 1

Up to Yellow Key
Area, Level 3

Mine 12—Yellow Key Area, Level 3

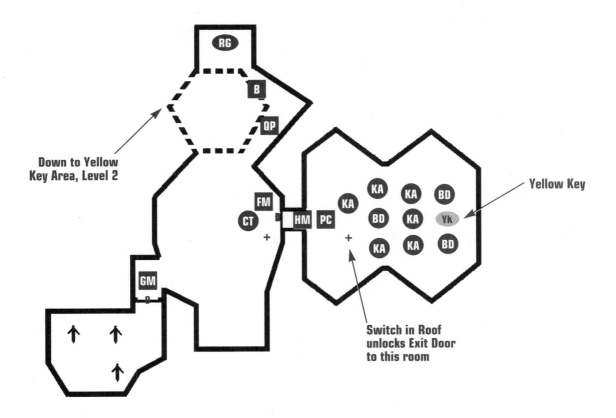

Down to Yellow
Key Area, Level 2

Yellow Key

Switch in Roof
unlocks Exit Door
to this room

Mine 12—Red Key Area, Level 1

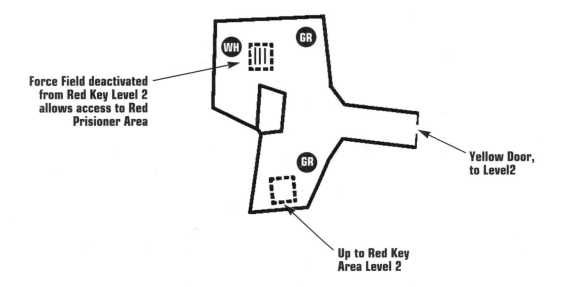

Force Field deactivated
from Red Key Level 2
allows access to Red
Prisioner Area

Yellow Door,
to Level2

Up to Red Key
Area Level 2

Mine 12—Red Prisoner Area

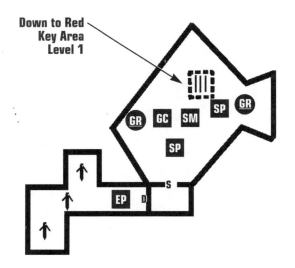

Down to Red
Key Area
Level 1

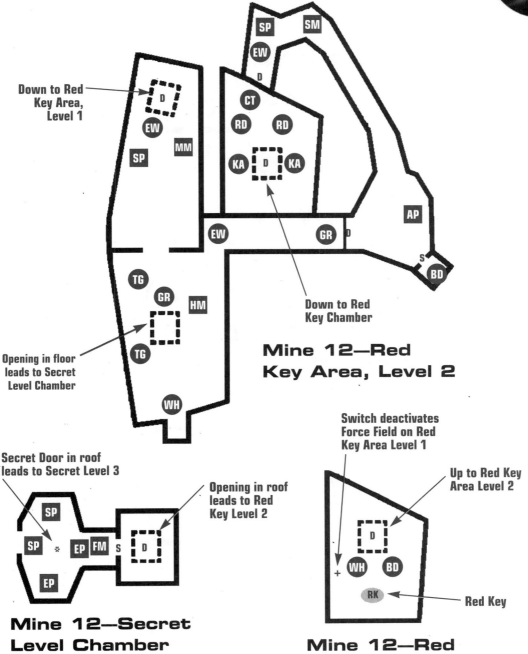

Down to Red
Key Area,
Level 1

Down to Red
Key Chamber

**Mine 12—Red
Key Area, Level 2**

Opening in floor
leads to Secret
Level Chamber

Switch deactivates
Force Field on Red
Key Area Level 1

Secret Door in roof
leads to Secret Level 3

Opening in roof
leads to Red
Key Level 2

Up to Red Key
Area Level 2

Red Key

**Mine 12—Secret
Level Chamber**

**Mine 12—Red
Key Chamber**

Mine 12—End-Boss Area

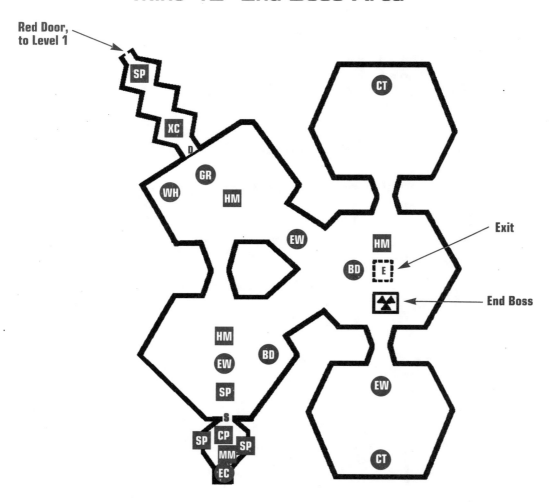

Red Door, to Level 1

Exit

End Boss

are two panels on each side of room, one panel in front of the force field and two panels behind a secret door above the force field.

Fly back to the large room. Go through the door used earlier to gain access to this room and make a left to the blue door. Once past the blue door, follow the passage all the way to the room with lava flowing down from the ceiling. Fly into and up the lava flow. Follow the passage until you come to a door. Fly though the door and retrieve the yellow key. On the ceiling above the door is a control panel that will unlock the door for you to get out.

Return to the blue door. Fly straight away from the blue door until the room opens up. Strafe left, then up, then reverse course. In essence, the yellow door is directly above the blue door. Once through the yellow door turn left, then go through the door in the ceiling and follow the tunnel all the way to the red key.

Return to the insertion point. Just below the door to insertion point is the red door. Hints on the Boss's armaments and techniques on how to destroy this Boss are listed in your Intelligence Reports.

Once you have defeated the Mine Boss, you can head for the exit or to the second secret level. To get to the secret level, go through the yellow door, then go up through the door in the ceiling. Fly to the next room with the grate at the bottom. Go down to grate and into room next to it. Shoot the secret door in ceiling and enter through the red portal.

If you just want to get out, the mine exit is located where the Boss robot is, in the ceiling of the center room furthest from the red door.

Mine 13—Sleetstone Tunnels

Turn right and destroy the door to free the Guidebot. Turn left and go through the door and you'll come to an intersection of grated corridors. Go down at that intersection and follow the passage. You'll find the blue key at the end of the passage.

Return to that same grated intersection, but instead of going down take the left passage. As you pass through the yellow door, you'll see three doors. Enter the door to the right. Follow the passage until you

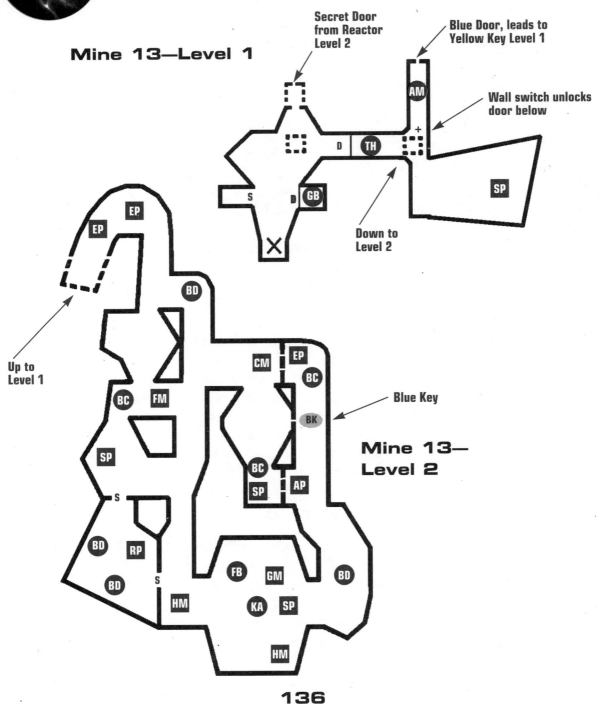

Mine 13—Level 1

Secret Door
from Reactor
Level 2

Blue Door, leads to
Yellow Key Level 1

AM

Wall switch unlocks
door below

D   TH

+

SP

D   GB

S

Down to
Level 2

X

EP

EP

Up to
Level 1

BD

CM   EP

BC

BC   FM

BK

Blue Key

Mine 13—
Level 2

SP

S

BC

SP   AP

BD   RP

S

BD

FB   GM   BD

HM

KA   SP

HM

Mine 13—Yellow Key Level 1

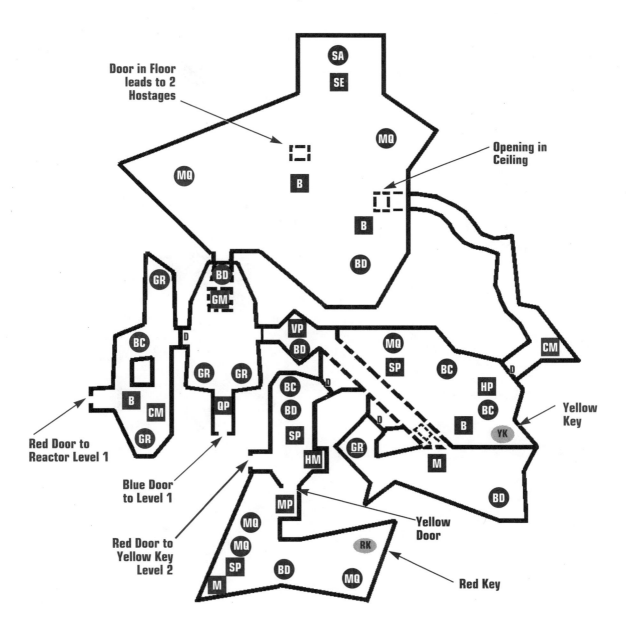

Door in Floor
leads to 2
Hostages

Opening in
Ceiling

Yellow
Key

Red Door to
Reactor Level 1

Blue Door
to Level 1

Red Door to
Yellow Key
Level 2

Yellow
Door

Red Key

Mine 13—Reactor Level 1

Mine 13—Yellow Key Level 2

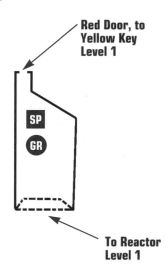

Red Door, to Yellow Key Level 1

SP

GR

To Reactor Level 1

Mine 13— Reactor Level 2

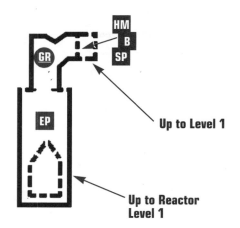

HM

B

SP

GR

Up to Level 1

EP

Up to Reactor Level 1

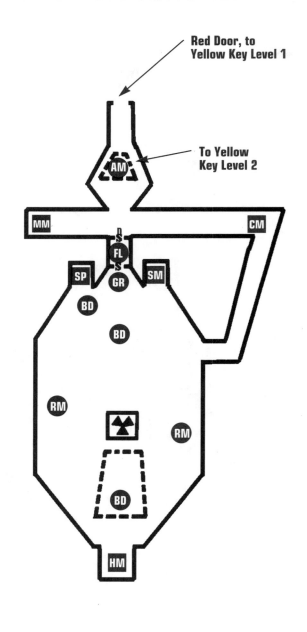

Red Door, to Yellow Key Level 1

To Yellow Key Level 2

AM

MM

CM

FL

SP

GR

SM

BD

BD

RM

RM

BD

HM

reach the large room made of grates and fences. Upon entering this room, search the upper level for the key. Go through the door to the left of the door you originally used to enter the room. You should now see both the red and yellow doors. Enter the yellow door. The red key is on the far side of the room in plain sight.

Go back to red door mentioned above and follow the passage to reactor. You know the drill.

Once the reactor explodes, a secret door opens giving you a short cut to the mine exit. Go through the secret door where you'll find a second red door. Pass through the red door and another door, then make a right. After passing through the blue door make a right at the next intersection. The exit is just past the next door, on the ceiling.

Mine 14—Arcticon Corridor

Follow the left wall. When you reach the chasm, the door to the Guidebot will be on the left side at the base of the chasm. Destroy door to release the Guidebot.

Return to the insertion point and follow the right wall. Enter the first door you encounter. This door opens up over a mine shaft. Go down the mine shaft and through the door at the bottom. From this door veer slightly left. You'll pass over a small trench and then have to ascend slightly over the next trench. When you reach the third trench, go straight down and retrieve the blue key.

From there keep traveling to the back of the room. On the left hand side there is a control panel. Destroy it. Go back to the door at the bottom of the mine shaft. If you are facing the door leading to the mine shaft, turn right and follow the wall on your left until you encounter a door. Go through the door until you come to three large rooms that are connected length-wise. About midway in the second room, there is a passage leading up and ending at a blue door. Beyond the blue door is a room which contains the yellow key. Be sure to hit the control panel at the back of the room, because it removes the grate on the floor.

Go through the door that the grate was covering, and the passage

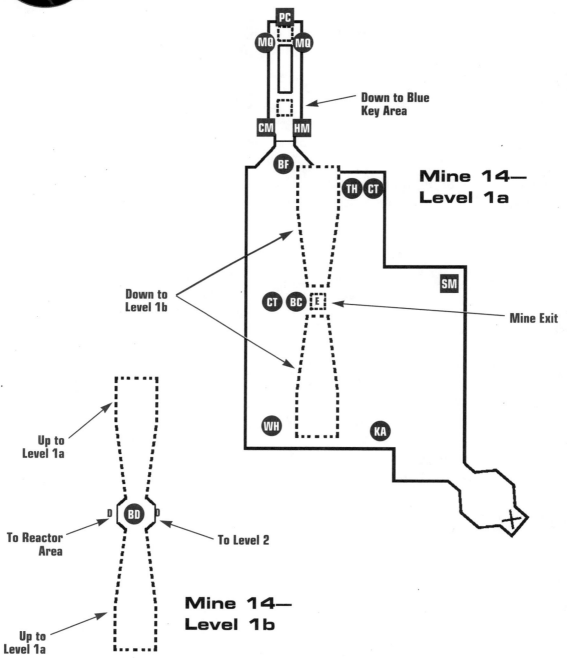

Down to Blue
Key Area

Mine 14—
Level 1a

Down to
Level 1b

Mine Exit

Up to
Level 1a

To Reactor
Area

To Level 2

Up to
Level 1a

Mine 14—
Level 1b

Mine 14—Level 2

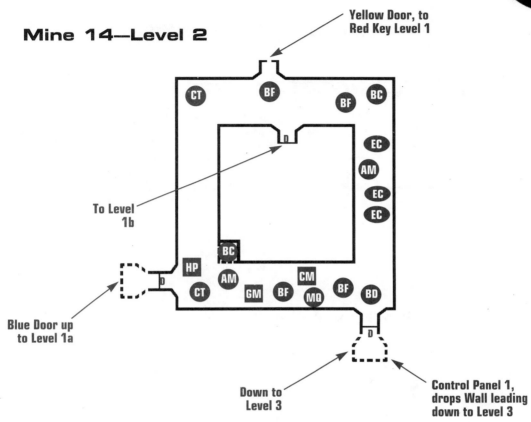

Yellow Door, to
Red Key Level 1

To Level
1b

Blue Door up
to Level 1a

Down to
Level 3

Control Panel 1,
drops Wall leading
down to Level 3

Mine 14—Level 3a

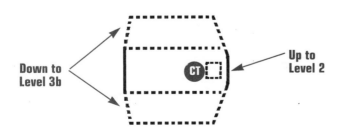

Down to
Level 3b

Up to
Level 2

Mine 14—Level 3b

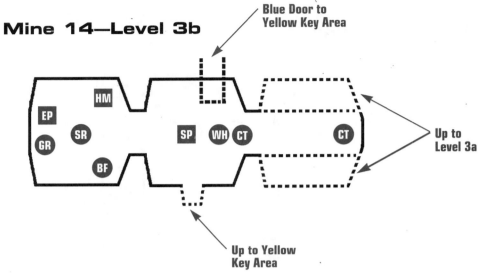

Blue Door to
Yellow Key Area

Up to
Level 3a

Up to Yellow
Key Area

Mine 14—Blue Key Area

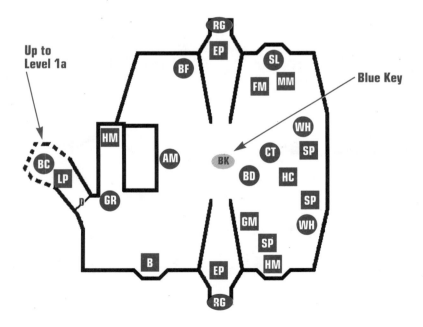

Up to
Level 1a

Blue Key

PART 2   Mission Maps

Mine 14— Yellow Key Area

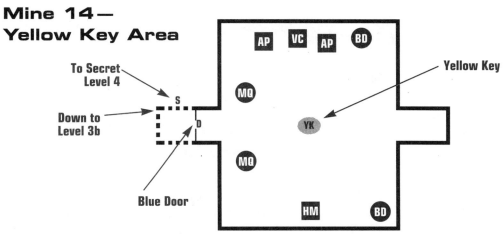

To Secret Level 4

Down to Level 3b

Blue Door

Yellow Key

Mine 14—Red Key Level 1

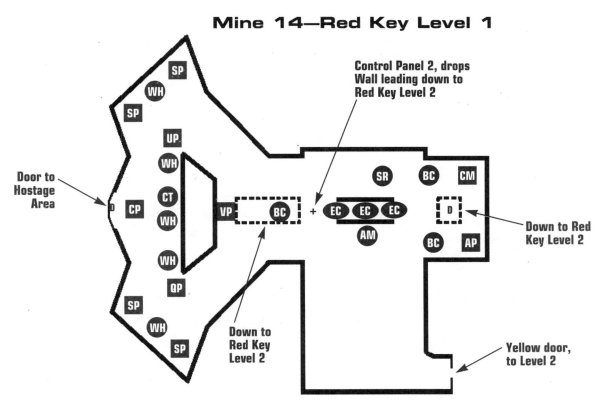

Control Panel 2, drops Wall leading down to Red Key Level 2

Door to Hostage Area

Down to Red Key Level 2

Down to Red Key Level 2

Yellow door, to Level 2

Mine 14—Red Key Level 2

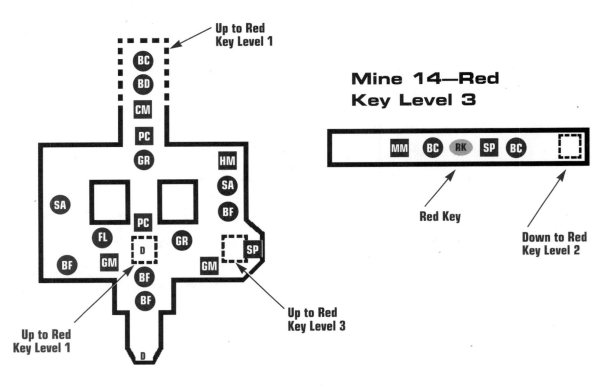

Up to Red
Key Level 1

BC

BD

CM

PC

GR

HM

SA

SA

BF

PC

FL

GR

D

SP

BF

GM

GM

BF

BF

Up to Red
Key Level 1

D

Up to Red
Key Level 3

Mine 14—Red Key Level 3

MM BC RK SP BC

Red Key

Down to Red
Key Level 2

Mine 14—Mine Reactor Area

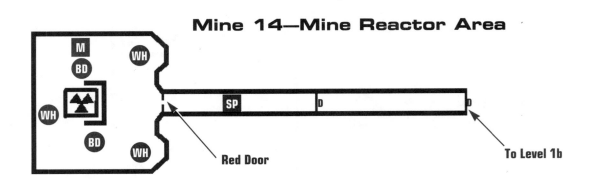

M

WH

BD

WH

SP D D

BD

WH

Red Door

To Level 1b

you find leads you through a force field corridor and then to a room with a yellow door. The yellow door is slightly to the left of your current passage. Take the yellow door and follow the right wall down until you find a doorway in the floor with a fusion cannon on the other side. Go through the door and circle around the ceiling. There will be an opening in one of the corners of the room. In the opening is a narrow passage leading to the red key.

Go through the only other door in the room. It will lead you across another force field bridge and then to a room with a control panel. Destroy the control panel and then search for the secret door next to it. Take the passage beyond the secret door all the way back to the room where the yellow key was. From this room take the red door to the reactor room and get ready to shoot.

When you blow the reactor take the red door and travel as straight as possible. As soon as you pass the door at the end of the force field corridor, stop! Slide left and then ascend. The exit will be in the center of the room in the ceiling.

Mine 15—Icehammer Caverns

Due to the level of darkness in this mine, and the relative distance to the first energy center you can encounter, energy management is crucial to successful completion. It is important to conserve your energy as much as possible and to regulate your use of headlights. Making and maintaining a safe path to the energy center will help prevent running out of energy in the middle of a firefight.

From your starting point, the second door you encounter will open to a large, subdivided chamber with a robot generator nestled in the ceiling. The best tactic to employ here is to enter far enough into the chamber to activate the generator, then retreat back into the doorway. The newly spawned robots will track you, and from this position it is possible to see the robots as they attack. Continue to alternatively pop into the chamber long enough for the robots to follow, and then duck back

Mine 15—Level 1

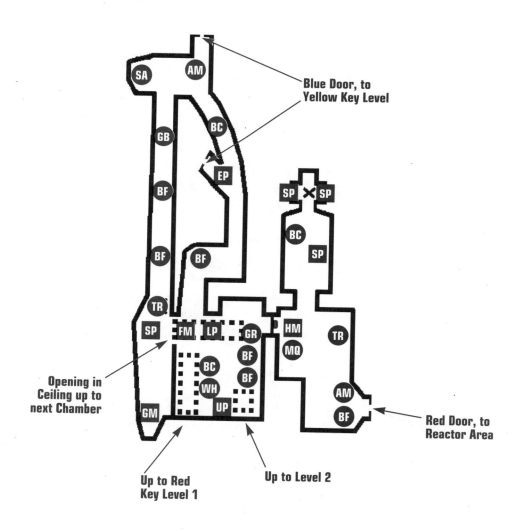

Blue Door, to
Yellow Key Level

Opening in
Ceiling up to
next Chamber

Up to Red
Key Level 1

Up to Level 2

Red Door, to
Reactor Area

Mine 15—Level 2

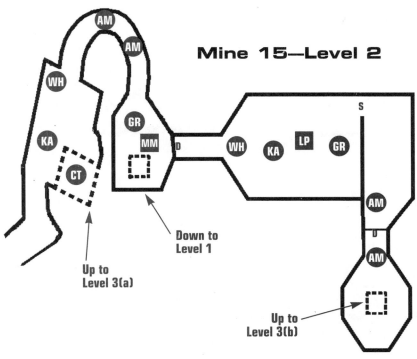

Down to
Level 1

Up to
Level 3(a)

Up to
Level 3(b)

Mine 15—Level 3

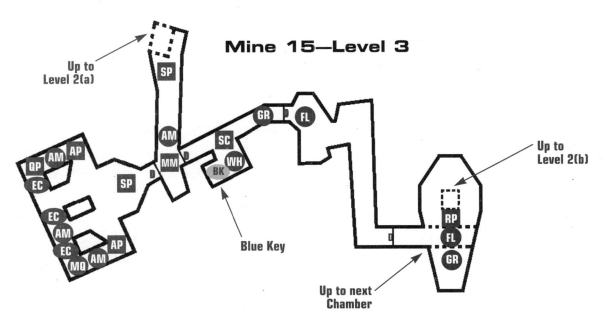

Up to
Level 2(a)

Up to
Level 2(b)

Blue Key

Up to next
Chamber

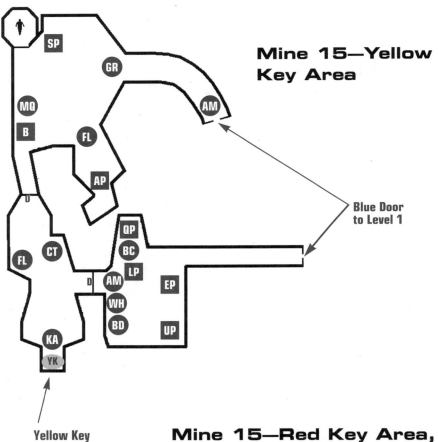

Mine 15—Yellow Key Area

Blue Door to Level 1

Yellow Key

Mine 15—Red Key Area, Level 1

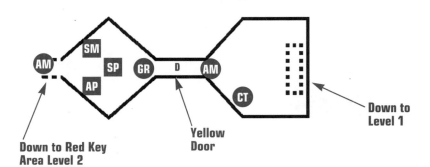

Down to Red Key Area Level 2

Yellow Door

Down to Level 1

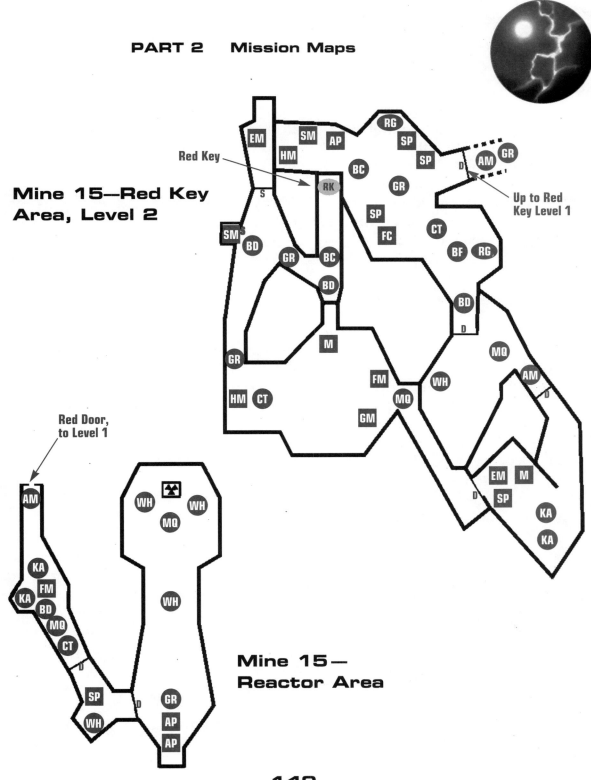

Red Key

Mine 15—Red Key
Area, Level 2

Up to Red
Key Level 1

Red Door,
to Level 1

Mine 15—
Reactor Area

into the doorway, maximizing cover while destroying all the robots. Once the robot generator has deactivated, it is then safe to continue.

Take the vertical shaft leading to level 2. From there take the vertical shaft to level 3 at point (a). Resistance along the way is moderate, but still use as much cover to your advantage as much as possible. Once you've reached level 3, proceed directly to the energy recharge center and recharge your weapons. Once there proceed to the Blue Key chamber and retrieve the key.

Retrace your steps to level 1 and continue to the blue door. Take the blue door closest to the hostage area, and continue to the Yellow Key chamber. This route will take you through the smallest concentration of enemy robots possible. Once you have the yellow key in your possession, go back to level 1 where the yellow door is located.

The room just beyond the yellow door has a light concentration of enemy robots, but the large chamber beyond this has a high collection of robots and 2 robot generators. Proceed into this chamber with extreme caution. Lead as many robots as possible into the doorway to this chamber and destroy them there, where cover is available. If you feel the desire to engage in a chaotic firefight out in the open, make sure to stay in motion at all times and not fly along a straight trajectory because the robots—especially missile bearing robots—will definitely track you, and track you accurately.

When this chamber is clear and the robot generators have deactivated, continue on to the location of the red key. Study the map carefully and expect Kamikazes charging you once you are through the third door you encounter past the red door. Utilize cover wherever possible as you make your way to the red key. When you make your way back, however, the 2 robot generators will reactivate when you return to the first large chamber you encountered on this level. At this stage, it would be best to simply use your afterburners and race to the doorway leading to level 1. Any robots that may have managed to maintain pursuit should be fairly easy to deal with once the door has closed.

At level 1 you will find the red door leading to the mine's reactor. The first chamber past this door should not pose a terrible problem if you make sure to shoot through the red door from a respectable distance away. Once inside the actual reactor chamber itself, you will find that the reactor core is at the far end as the chamber slopes down in elevation. Use this slope to your advantage, and maintain a barrage at the reactor from as far away as possible. Once the reactor is blown, proceed to the first chamber on this reactor level that is past the red door; this is where the exit is. In the chamber immediately preceding it, a secret door in the ceiling will be triggered by the destruction of the reactor, releasing 2 Grizzlies. So long as you know when to expect them, they should not pose a significant threat to you. You will find the mine exit in the next chamber, recessed into the ceiling and close to the door.

Mine 16—Terrafrost Catacombs

From the starting point go through the first immediate door to the vertical opening that leads down to level 2. From there, resistance is stiff, but not insurmountable as you proceed to the vertical shaft that leads down to level 3. You will notice that at the very bottom of the shaft is a door leading to a small room with an energy center. Make careful note of this location because you will need to come back to it later for recharging. From there, keep going on to level 3b where there is a large vertical shaft leading to level 4. This long shaft has multiple ledges along it's length, preventing you from taking a straight trajectory up to the very top. Use these ledges for cover since there are multiple robots hiding on each ledge.

At the top, you will find a door leading to the blue key chamber. This chamber is filled with enemy robots, so make sure to pick each of them off, one at a time from the doorway—the alternative is that they will rush you the instant you appear inside the chamber.

Once the blue key is in your possession, continue on to the blue door. This next chamber is moderately populated with robots, but has a robot generator. The best tactic is, again, to maximize your cover from behind the doorway and pick them off one by one. Alternatively, it is

possible to charge straight down into the vertical shaft that leads down to yellow key level 2. This is possible, but the downside is that there will be a large multitude of robots waiting for you there when you have to pass by this way again.

When you reach the yellow key at level 3, you will notice that it is contained within two sets of forces fields. The control panel that deactivates them is on the other side of the force fields, forcing you to shoot through them to deactivate them. As long as all of the robots in the immediate vicinity have been cleared, this should not be a problem.

After you retrieve the yellow key, continue on towards level 1 by retracing your steps and continuing through the blue door that leads to level 1. Once there, take the vertical shaft that leads to red key level 1. At this point proceed very cautiously. Beyond the yellow door there is a short tunnel that opens up to the a very large vertical opening. From the safety of the short tunnel you must destroy all of the robots in order to have a reasonable chance to retrieve the red key and make it back.

At red key level 2, go on to the vertical shaft leading up to red key level 3. At this point there are two ways to retrieve the key. You can patiently destroy every robot from the relative safety of the vertical shaft, or you can charge into the chamber with afterburners, retrieve the key, then race back down the shaft. Either way will work, but if you are low on shields, the more patient tactic is appropriate.

With the red key in your possession, proceed to level 3b, where the red door is located. Beyond this door, you will find a vertical opening with an energy center along its length. From this location, destroy as many of the robots in the adjacent room as possible. Once you have done so successfully, you have a shot at the Mine Boss. This is best achieved by fast, hit-and-run tactics, and never staying in one place or holding a continuous trajectory. This Boss fires flash missiles, and once the Boss successfully blinds you, it is very easy for him to keep you blind until you are dead.

When you have successfully destroyed this Boss, continue on through the short remaining maze to the exit.

Mine 16—Level 1

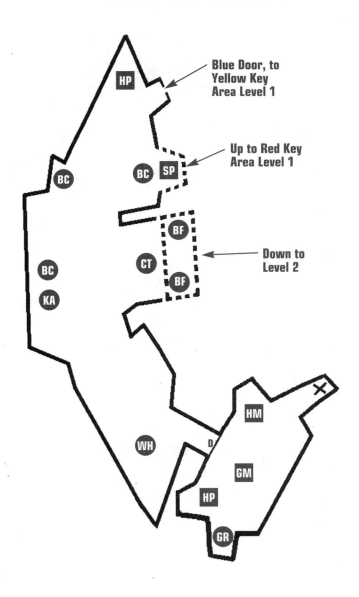

Blue Door, to Yellow Key Area Level 1

Up to Red Key Area Level 1

Down to Level 2

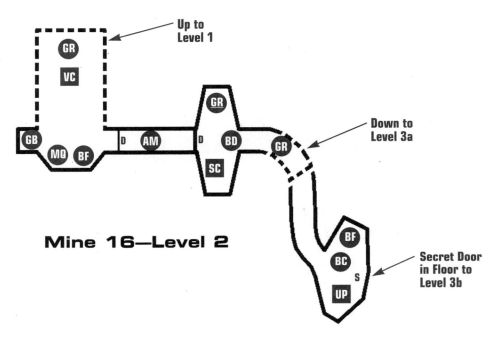

Up to
Level 1

Down to
Level 3a

Mine 16—Level 2

Secret Door
in Floor to
Level 3b

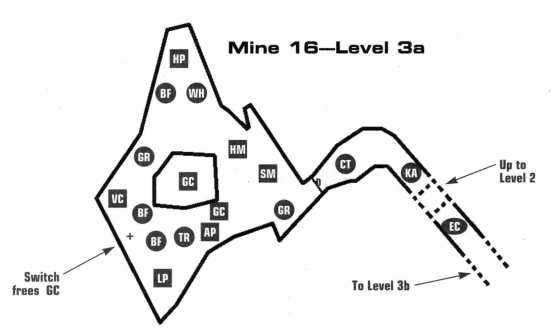

Mine 16—Level 3a

Up to
Level 2

Switch
frees GC

To Level 3b

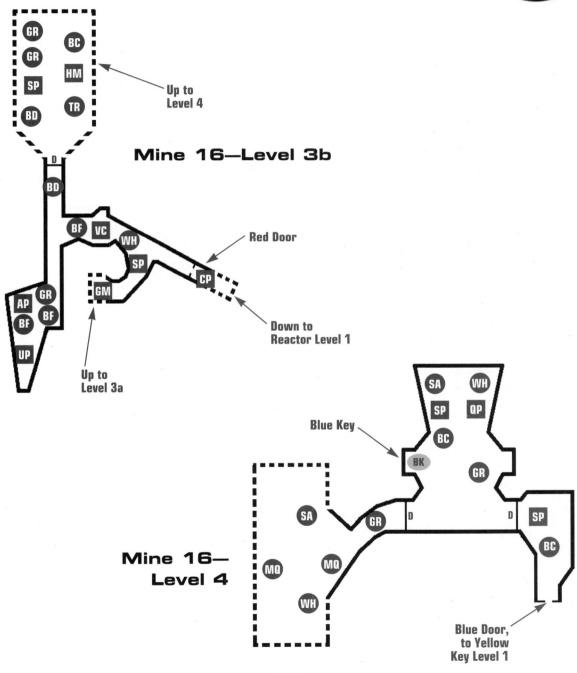

Mine 16—Level 3b

Up to Level 4

Red Door

Down to Reactor Level 1

Up to Level 3a

Mine 16— Level 4

Blue Key

Blue Door, to Yellow Key Level 1

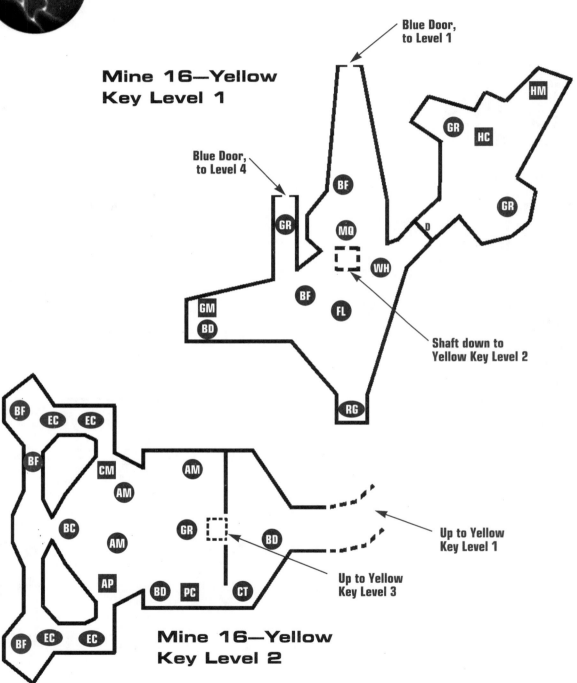

Blue Door,
to Level 1

**Mine 16—Yellow
Key Level 1**

HM

GR

HC

Blue Door,
to Level 4

BF

GR

GR

MQ

D

WH

Shaft down to
Yellow Key Level 2

BF

GM

FL

BD

RG

BF

EC

EC

BF

CM

AM

AM

Up to Yellow
Key Level 1

BC

GR

AM

BD

AP

BD

PC

CT

Up to Yellow
Key Level 3

BF

EC

EC

**Mine 16—Yellow
Key Level 2**

156

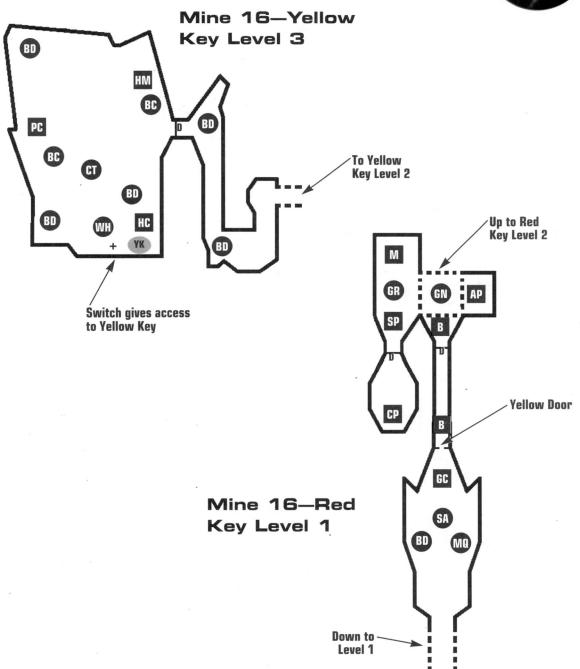

Mine 16—Yellow Key Level 3

BD

HM
BC

PC

BC
CT

BD

BD
WH   HC

+   YK

BD

D
BD

BD

To Yellow Key Level 2

Switch gives access to Yellow Key

M

GR   GN   AP

SP   B

CP

Up to Red Key Level 2

Yellow Door

B

GC

SA

BD   MQ

Mine 16—Red Key Level 1

Down to Level 1

Mine 16—Red Key Level 2

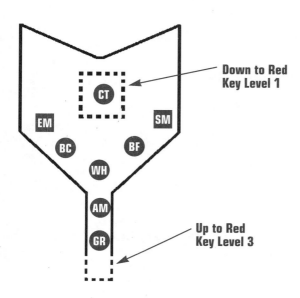

Down to Red Key Level 1

Up to Red Key Level 3

Mine 16—Red Key Level 3

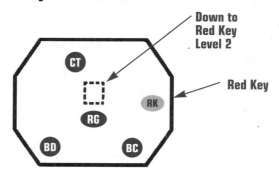

Down to Red Key Level 2

Red Key

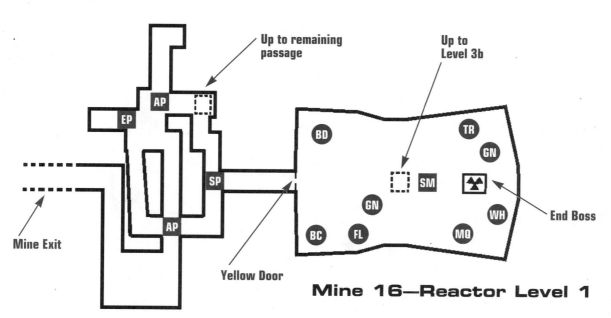

Up to remaining passage

Up to Level 3b

End Boss

Mine Exit

Yellow Door

Mine 16—Reactor Level 1

Mine 17 — y'tor III

This mine poses unusual challenges in the form of puzzles. The first, and least obvious, is the blue key.

The blue key is not contained in one specific location, it is housed inside of a robot. A modified blue Kamikaze flits through the mine. When it is destroyed, the blue key will appear at the spot where it died. The best way to handle this situation is to fly through and clear the initial levels of enemy robots and to familiarize yourself with the layout of this mine. Once this is done, either wait in one place or fly around randomly until you run into this robot. This robot, however, is extremely fast and maneuverable, and will require a well-aimed shot to be destroyed.

When you have the blue key, proceed through level 2 to the blue door. Once there continue on until you reach the yellow key area. This area is a trap. As soon as you've cleared this area of enemies and have acquired the yellow key, a door in the ceiling will open discharging Energy Wasps. If you venture down the vertical shaft where the yellow key was located, a door that cannot be opened will close over the chamber's entrance. The best way to deal with this is to not go down the vertical shaft where the yellow key was located.

When you exit this chamber, you will find that there is another such door just before the blue door. The best way to handle this is to approach closely this door, then turn around and go back the way you came. You should see a control panel behind a secret door that has opened. Destroy this and the door will be opened.

Continue down to the red key area. You will find resistance from a number of Energy Wasps, Tigers, and others. Although these robots will pose a problem, attaining the red key is far more straight forward than attaining the blue key.

The moment the red key is in your possession, a whole section of wall on level 2 will drop away, revealing the red door to the reactor room. Fly through it, and you will come across an opening in the floor where a robot generator is located. Destroy all of the robots emerging to attack you, then continue to where the reactor core is actually situated.

When the reactor is destroyed, you will find the red door cannot be

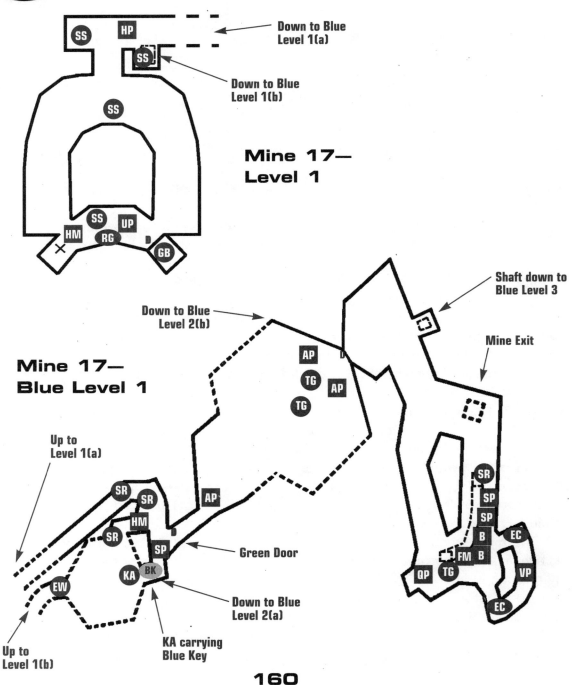

Down to Blue
Level 1(a)

Down to Blue
Level 1(b)

Mine 17—
Level 1

Shaft down to
Blue Level 3

Down to Blue
Level 2(b)

Mine Exit

Mine 17—
Blue Level 1

Up to
Level 1(a)

Green Door

Down to Blue
Level 2(a)

KA carrying
Blue Key

Up to
Level 1(b)

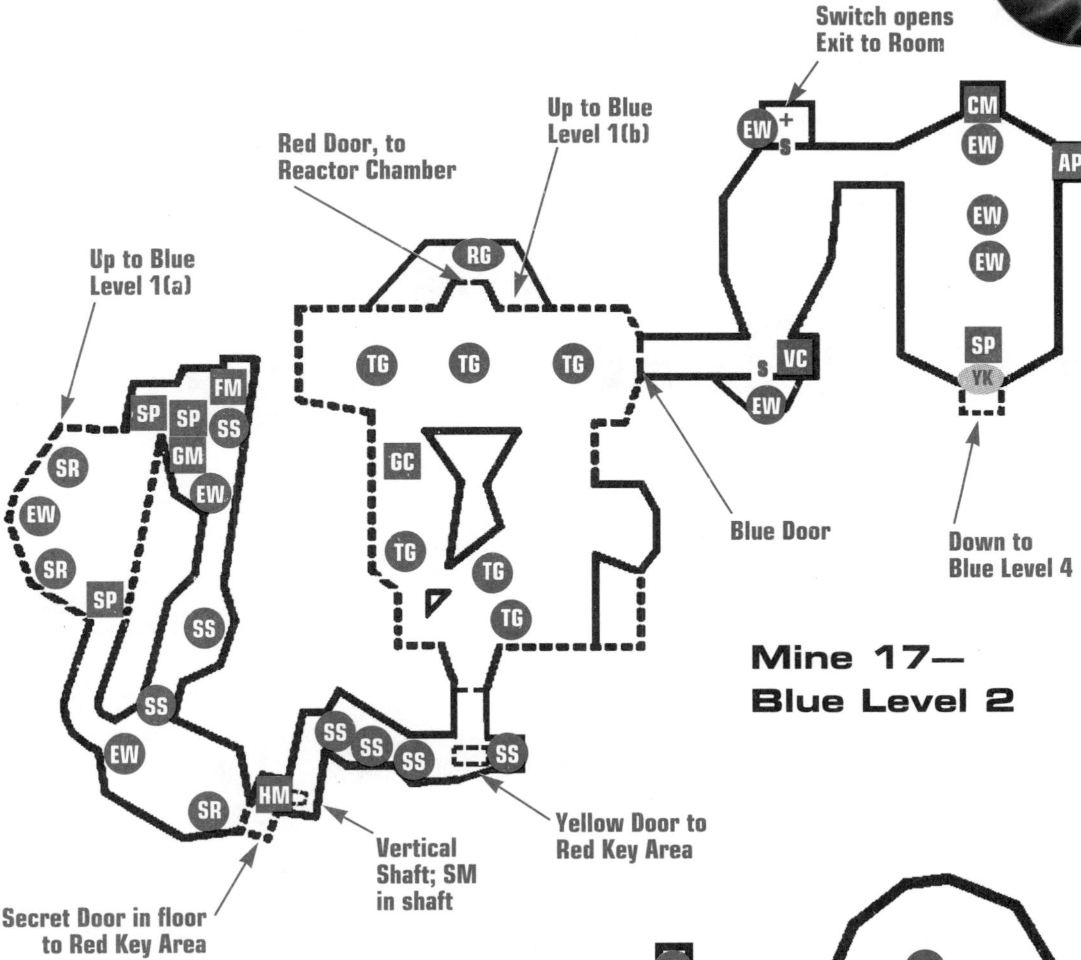

Switch opens Exit to Room

EW +
S

CM
EW
AP
EW
EW
SP
VK

Up to Blue Level 1(b)

Red Door, to Reactor Chamber

RG

Up to Blue Level 1(a)

TG   TG   TG

FM
SP   SP   SS
SR   GM
EW   EW
SR
SP

GC

TG

TG

TG

S   VC
EW

Blue Door

Down to Blue Level 4

Mine 17— Blue Level 2

SS

SS

EW

SR   HM

SS   SS   SS   SS
SS

Yellow Door to Red Key Area

Vertical Shaft; SM in shaft

Secret Door in floor to Red Key Area

EW

HM

MI
SM   HP   MI
SR
SP
MI   SM
GM

SP

SP   MI

EW   VP

+   SP   SP

To Secret Level 5   *   S

Up to Blue Level 2

Wall Switch opens entrance to adjacent Room

EP
S
EW

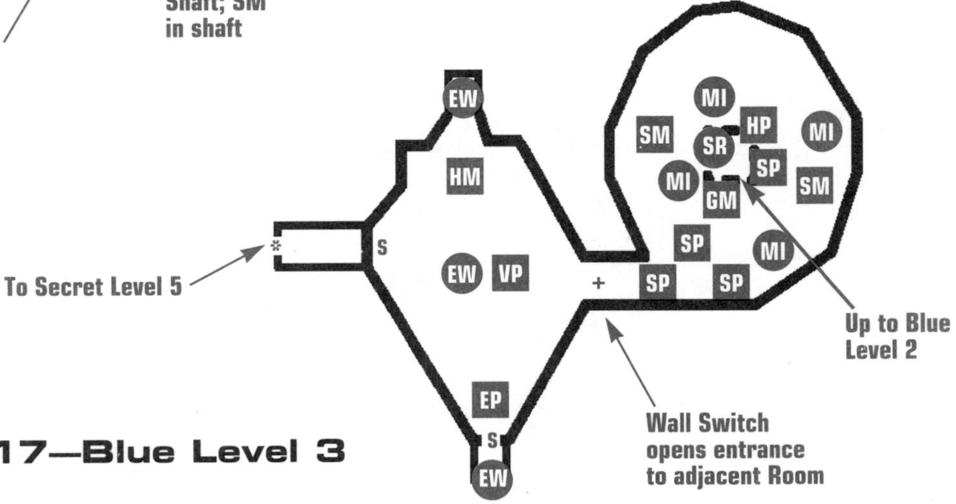

Mine 17—Blue Level 3

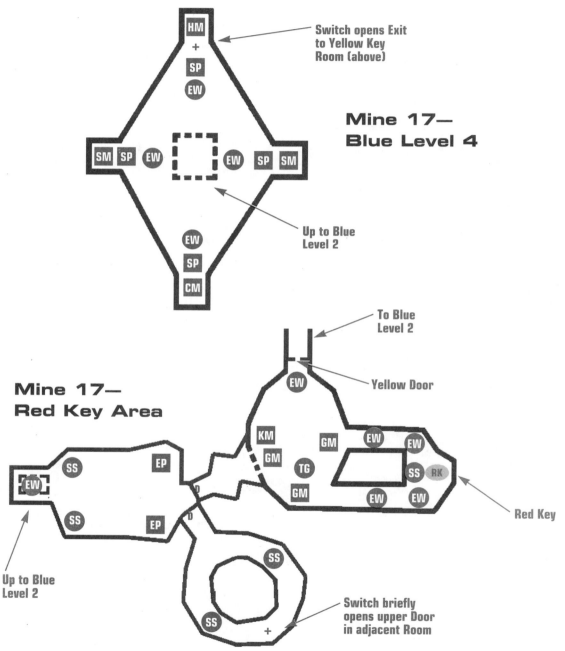

Switch opens Exit
to Yellow Key
Room (above)

Mine 17—
Blue Level 4

Up to Blue
Level 2

To Blue
Level 2

Yellow Door

Mine 17—
Red Key Area

Red Key

Up to Blue
Level 2

Switch briefly
opens upper Door
in adjacent Room

Mine 17—Reactor Chamber

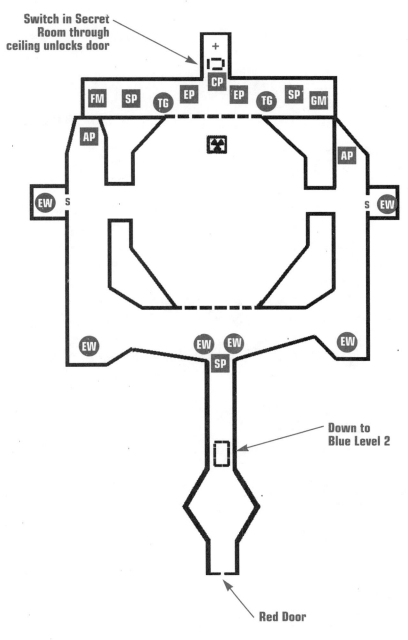

Switch in Secret Room through ceiling unlocks door

Down to Blue Level 2

Red Door

opened from the inside. Instead, you must destroy all of the robots blocking your path, then fly down into the vertical opening that contains the robot generator. You will find that this depression opens up into a passageway that leads directly to Level 2. From there ascend to Level 1 then fight your way to the mine exit area. This should be guarded by a cloaked Tiger, but with the afterburner you should be able to bypass him if you're not in a condition to fight.

Mine 18—Drec'Nilbie K'luh

Your starting point in this mine is almost immediately compromised by the fact that there are enemy robots within the large, open chamber you start in. As you engage them, remember to constantly keep moving and not give them a solid trajectory that they can track. Once this immediate threat is dealt with, fly down to level 2, and proceed through the door that leads to the blue key area.

There are many robots along this particular passageway, so make sure to take the time to kill each one individually and not let them get together into groups. Near the blue key level, you will see two vertical shafts leading the way. Either one will lead up to the blue key chamber. After you've retrieved the blue key and destroyed the two robots there, retrace your steps and go back to level 1. Care should be exercised, however. The route back is littered once again by robots that have been released from secret alcoves in the walls.

Once at level 1, fly through the blue door, then take the passageway that leads to yellow key level 2. Here your biggest threat is two cloaked Spartans. Once they and the rest of the robots are taken care of, you need to get the yellow key.

The yellow key is contained at the top of a pillar with a grate on one side of the tiny room, and a door on the other that can only be opened from the inside. The only way to get this key out is to position yourself by the grate so that when you fire your weapons, the shots will go through the grate and hit the door. Once the door gets triggered you have only a few seconds to fly all the way to the other side of the pillar, and get inside the yellow key room before the door closes.

Mine 18—Level 1

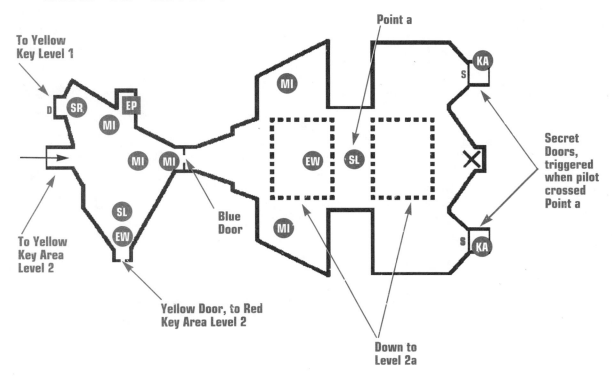

To Yellow Key Level 1

Point a

D

SR

EP

MI

MI

MI

MI

MI

KA

S

EW

SL

Secret Doors, triggered when pilot crossed Point a

S

KA

SL

EW

Blue Door

MI

To Yellow Key Area Level 2

Yellow Door, to Red Key Area Level 2

Down to Level 2a

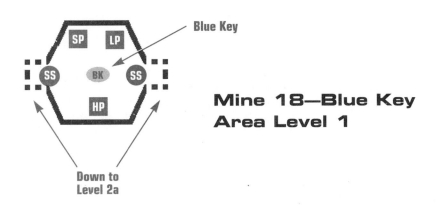

Blue Key

SP

LP

SS

BK

SS

HP

Mine 18—Blue Key Area Level 1

Down to Level 2a

Mine 18—Level 2a

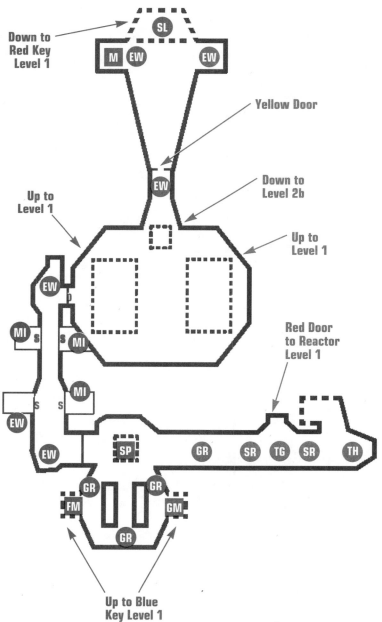

Down to
Red Key
Level 1

Yellow Door

Up to
Level 1

Down to
Level 2b

Up to
Level 1

Red Door
to Reactor
Level 1

Up to Blue
Key Level 1

Mine 18—Level 2b

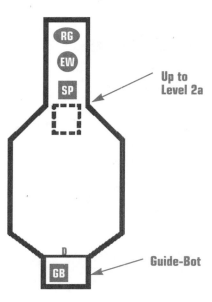

Up to
Level 2a

Guide-Bot

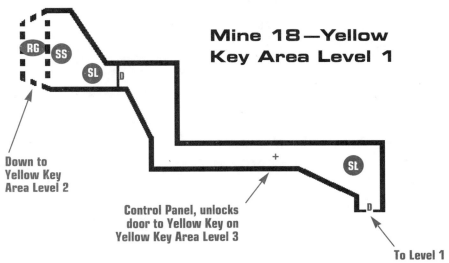

Mine 18—Yellow
Key Area Level 1

Down to
Yellow Key
Area Level 2

Control Panel, unlocks
door to Yellow Key on
Yellow Key Area Level 3

To Level 1

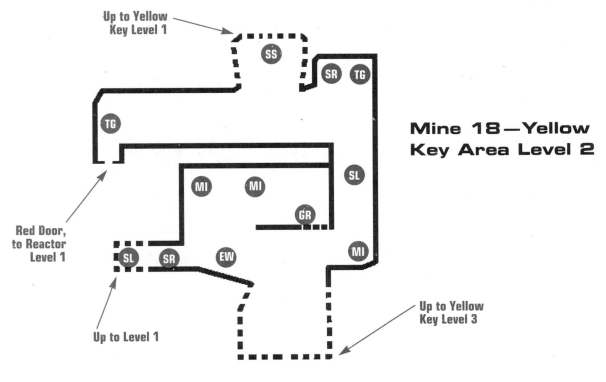

Up to Yellow
Key Level 1

Mine 18—Yellow
Key Area Level 2

Red Door,
to Reactor
Level 1

Up to Level 1

Up to Yellow
Key Level 3

Yellow Key

Shoot through
Grate to open Door

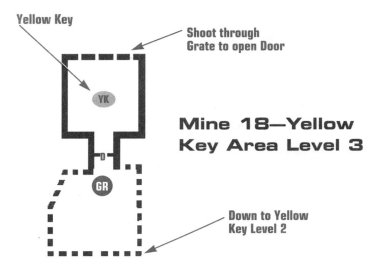

Mine 18—Yellow
Key Area Level 3

Down to Yellow
Key Level 2

Mine 18—Red Key Area Level 1

Up to Red
Key Level 2

Up to Red
Key Level 2

Up to
Level 2a

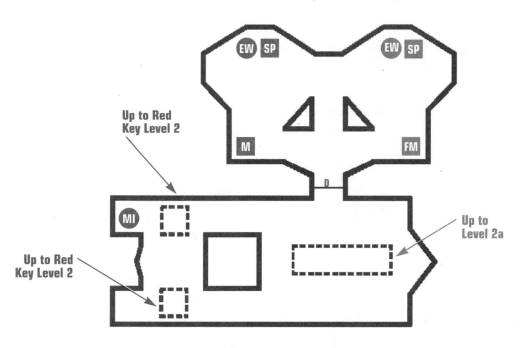

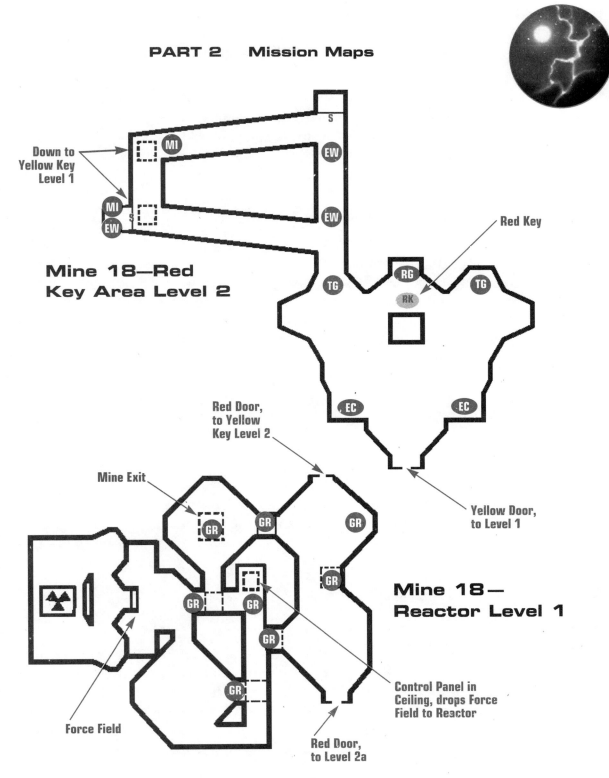

Down to
Yellow Key
Level 1

MI

MI
S
EW

**Mine 18—Red
Key Area Level 2**

S

EW

EW

Red Key

RG

TG   RK   TG

EC   EC

Red Door,
to Yellow
Key Level 2

Mine Exit

GR   GR   GR

GR

Yellow Door,
to Level 1

GR   GR   GR

GR

GR

**Mine 18—
Reactor Level 1**

Control Panel in
Ceiling, drops Force
Field to Reactor

Force Field

Red Door,
to Level 2a

Once you have the yellow key, proceed to red key level 1. Here you must fight the robots from the safety of the door because there is not enough room for maneuvers. When the red key is in your possession, retrace your steps until you have gotten to the end of yellow key level 1 where there is a robot generator and a red door.

Once the robot generator has been deactivated and all its robots are dead, you will be ready to enter past the red door. Inside are a host of robots that must be destroyed before you can do anything else. Use the cover of the door to aid you in this. When the robots are dead, find the control panel that is on the ceiling of one of the vertical alcoves. When you destroy this control panel, the force fields blocking off access to the reactor core will drop, leaving you free to fire upon the reactor. Before you do this, however, be sure that you have located the mine exit, which is also located in one of those vertical alcoves somewhere on reactor level 1. When the reactor goes, your immediate path may be blocked by robots emerging from behind secret chambers on the level, but a burst of the afterburner should help you navigate past them with hardly a scratch.

Mine 19—Nep-Hilim S'crub

Exit the chamber where you begin by taking the passage to the left of your starting position. You will enter another chamber with a long light panel across the ceiling. In this chamber, take the first passage to the left. Do not head down the corridor directly in front of you (despite the gleam of blue in the distance, the corridor straight ahead won't take you there). Instead, circumnavigate the room by following the steel grate wall that lies in front of you around to the left. It will carry you to the opposite side of the chamber and allow you to claim the blue key.

Once you've secured the blue key, return back the way you came, this time hugging the right wall of the corridor. Stop when you reach an alcove along the wall. Shoot the floor to open the secret door and descend into the shaft. Exit the shaft at the bottom and fly straight to the opposite side of the room. You will see a blue door; shoot it open and fly directly at the yellow key that will be floating in space.

Mine 19—Level 1

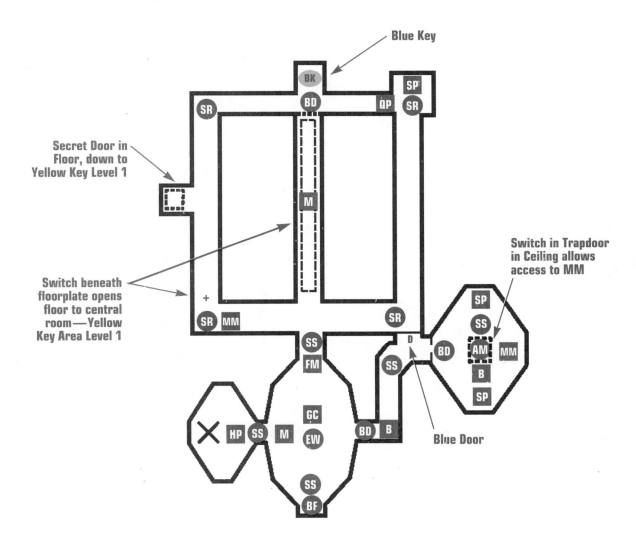

Blue Key

Secret Door in Floor, down to Yellow Key Level 1

Switch beneath floorplate opens floor to central room—Yellow Key Area Level 1

Switch in Trapdoor in Ceiling allows access to MM

Blue Door

DESCENT II The Official Strategy Guide

Mine 19—Yellow Key Area Level 1

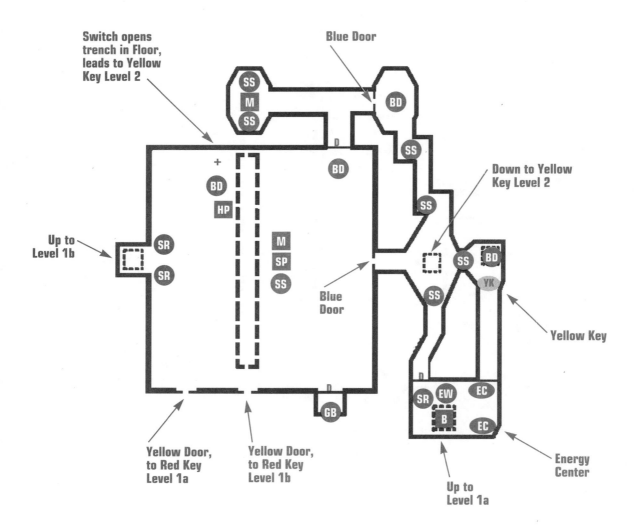

Switch opens trench in Floor, leads to Yellow Key Level 2

Blue Door

Down to Yellow Key Level 2

Up to Level 1b

Yellow Key

Blue Door

Up to Level 1a

Energy Center

Yellow Door, to Red Key Level 1a

Yellow Door, to Red Key Level 1b

172

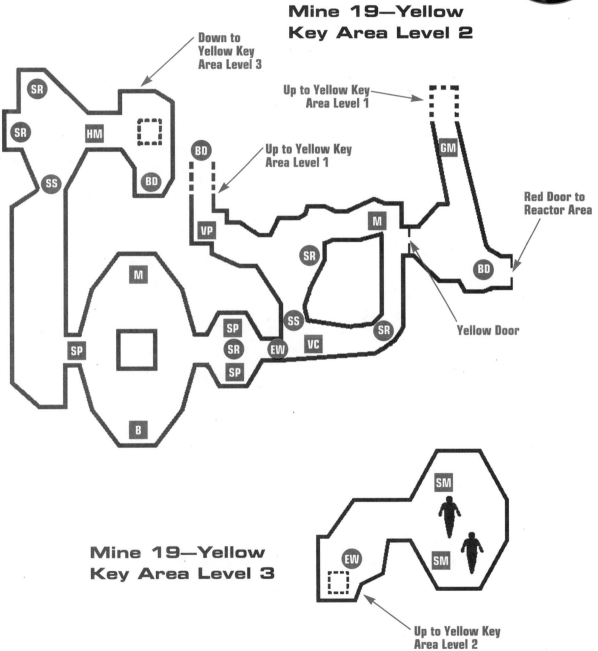

Mine 19—Yellow Key Area Level 2

Down to Yellow Key Area Level 3

SR

SR

HM

SS

BD

Up to Yellow Key Area Level 1

BD

Up to Yellow Key Area Level 1

GM

VP

Red Door to Reactor Area

M

M

SR

BD

SP

SS

Yellow Door

SP

SR

EW

VC

SR

SP

B

Mine 19—Yellow Key Area Level 3

SM

SM

EW

Up to Yellow Key Area Level 2

Mine 19—Red Key Area Level 1

Mine 19—Red Key Area Level 2

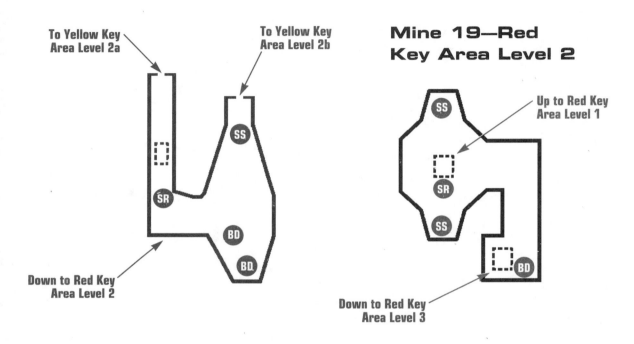

To Yellow Key Area Level 2a

To Yellow Key Area Level 2b

Down to Red Key Area Level 2

Up to Red Key Area Level 1

Down to Red Key Area Level 3

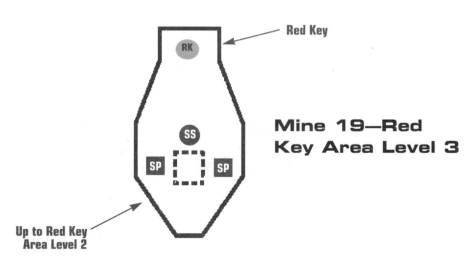

Red Key

Mine 19—Red Key Area Level 3

Up to Red Key Area Level 2

Mine 19—Reactor Area

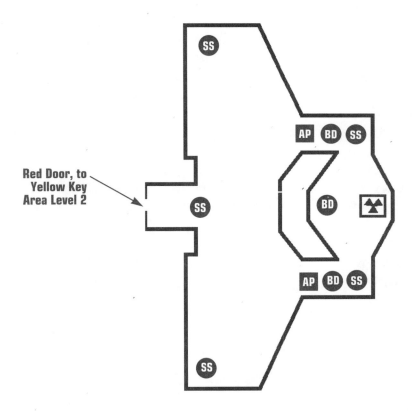

Red Door, to
Yellow Key
Area Level 2

Note: It is a good idea to mark the yellow key area, as you will pass through it two more times to complete the mission.

Now that you have the yellow key, backtrack through the blue door you entered and fly into the vast chamber beyond. Bear to the left and use flares and light sources to find the Guidebot's cage on the left wall of the chamber. Free the Guidebot.

Go to the top yellow door in the chamber (there are two yellow doors in the chamber, and you want the highest one on the wall). Open the door, then fly down the shaft and level-out into the room. Take the only exit corridor from the room, bear right around a corner, and then keep heading downwards until you reach the lava chamber. The red key floats in one of the alcoves.

Backtrack up the shafts to the yellow door you entered, then head through it and back into the large room. From here, go back to the blue door (it should be down and to the right as you leave the yellow door) and fly back to the exact area where you got the yellow key. At this point, fly straight down, level out and follow the corridor into a room with a red door.

Open the red door and fly to the back of the chamber. Blast the reactor into scrap metal.

Backtrack to the red door, hang a right, and head up the shaft you used to get into this area. Return to the small room where you retrieved the yellow key. From there, turn and head for the room with the blue door. The exit is in the ceiling.

Mine 20—Gytowt Station

In a hole directly in front of you is the cage with your Guidebot. To tantalize you, the blue key floats in a cage to the left. You start with a robot generator directly overhead, so be careful. Open the door directly in front of you (you can't open the one to the right anyway . . . yet), and turn left down the passage. The passage will make another left turn; bear with it until you dip down into a triangular shaped chamber.

In this chamber there will be a door to your left. Open it, drop down the shaft, and head for the corridor at the bottom. This corridor takes you to a shaft that leads directly up to the blue key.

Once you have the blue key, the cage opens and you are allowed to re-enter the starting room. Once there, exit out the same door you left before and follow your path back to the triangle room. This time, ignore the door on the left and fly to the opposite side of the room, then up into another corridor. Follow it around until you encounter a blue door on the left.

Open the blue door and hug the wall to the right to circumnavigate the large room beyond the door. You will pass over three lava pits set into the floor, as well as a yellow door to the right. Ignore them for the moment and concentrate on getting to the door on the right just after the yellow door.

Once you reach that door, you will see the yellow key floating beyond a force field, and a narrow shaft leading down. You'll need to find the control panel to shut off the field, so take the shaft down. Once down, you'll have three ways to go. One way leads right through a robot gener-ator (don't take that one). With your back oriented to the generator, follow the wall in front of you around to the left or right until you get behind the wall mass. When you do, you'll see a control panel behind a grate. Shoot through the bars of the grate to destroy the panel. The field around the yellow key will deactivate. Retrace your steps, head up the shaft, and grab the key to get yellow access.

Turn and face the door. Open it and go back out into the room with the three lava pits. Follow the wall around to the left until you reach the yellow door and open it. You will find yourself in a room that leads up. Halfway up on the far wall is the red access door. Ignore it and keep going up.

At the top of the room, follow the curving corridor around until you reach a door. Open it, then rush into the room and grab the red key.

Return through the door you came in to get to the red key room (the other doors will not open for you yet). Go back down the curving corri-dor, then halfway down the shaft to reach the red door. Open it. On the opposite wall beyond the door is a robot generator and on the floor in front of you is a shaft down.

On the level just below you is another red door that will lead to an

DESCENT II The Official Strategy Guide

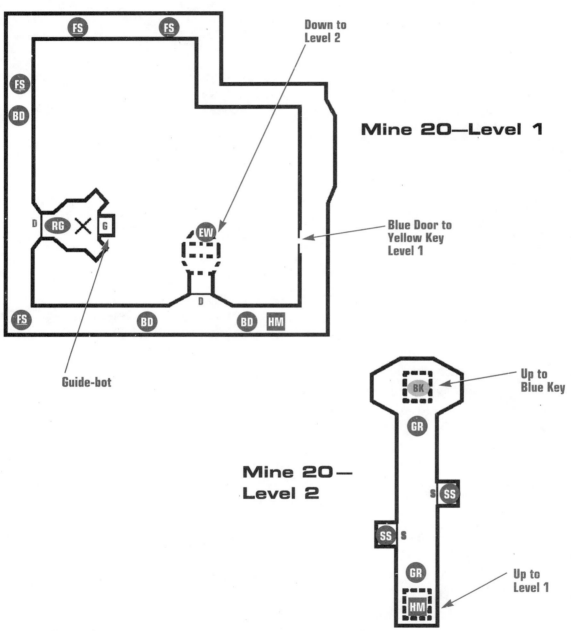

Down to Level 2

Mine 20—Level 1

Blue Door to Yellow Key Level 1

Guide-bot

Up to Blue Key

Mine 20— Level 2

Up to Level 1

178

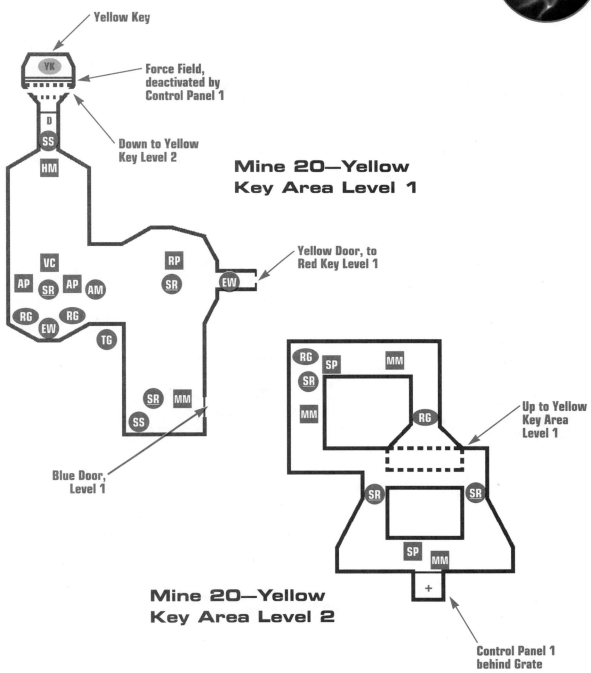

Yellow Key

Force Field,
deactivated by
Control Panel 1

Down to Yellow
Key Level 2

Mine 20—Yellow
Key Area Level 1

Yellow Door, to
Red Key Level 1

Up to Yellow
Key Area
Level 1

Blue Door,
Level 1

Mine 20—Yellow
Key Area Level 2

Control Panel 1
behind Grate

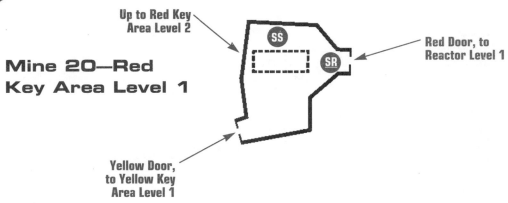

Mine 20—Red Key Area Level 1

Up to Red Key Area Level 2

Red Door, to Reactor Level 1

Yellow Door, to Yellow Key Area Level 1

Mine 20—Red Key Area Level 2

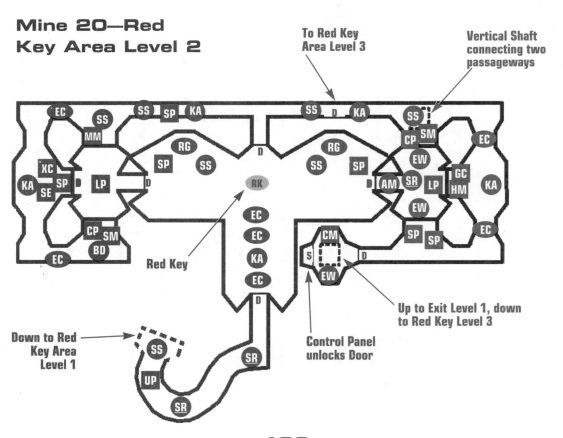

To Red Key Area Level 3

Vertical Shaft connecting two passageways

Red Key

Down to Red Key Area Level 1

Control Panel unlocks Door

Up to Exit Level 1, down to Red Key Level 3

Mine 20—Reactor Level 1

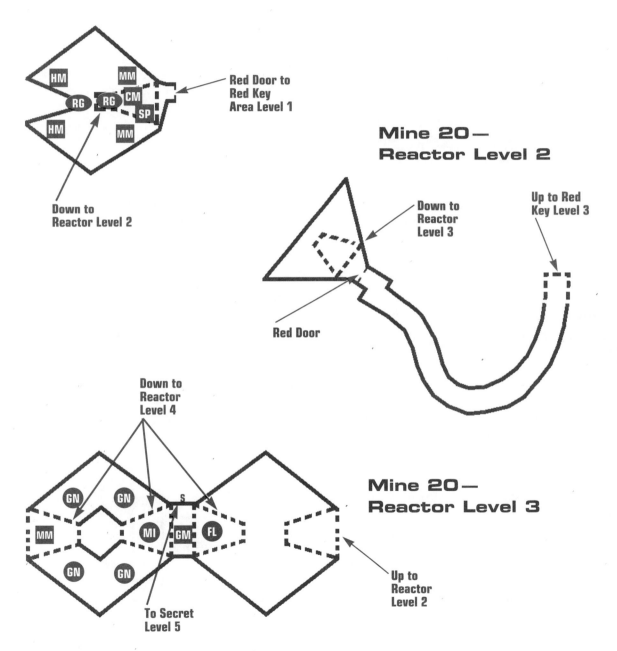

Red Door to
Red Key
Area Level 1

Down to
Reactor Level 2

Mine 20—
Reactor Level 2

Up to Red
Key Level 3

Down to
Reactor
Level 3

Red Door

Down to
Reactor
Level 4

Mine 20—
Reactor Level 3

Up to
Reactor
Level 2

To Secret
Level 5

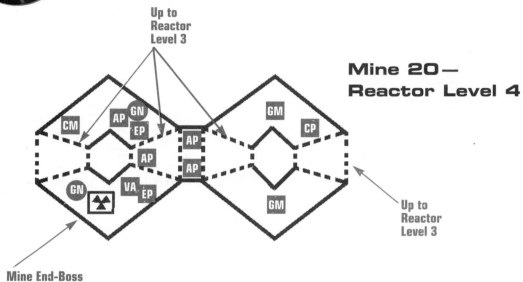

Up to
Reactor
Level 3

Mine 20—
Reactor Level 4

Up to
Reactor
Level 3

Mine End-Boss

Mine 20—Red
Key Area Level 3

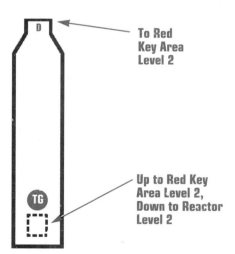

To Red
Key Area
Level 2

Up to Red Key
Area Level 2,
Down to Reactor
Level 2

Mine 20—
Exit Level 1

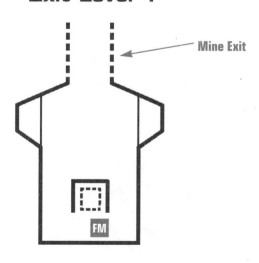

Mine Exit

exit. Pass it by for now and keep descending. The next two levels below the second red door are laid out like two joined octagons, with plenty of room for hit and run tactics. You'll need 'em because this is where you'll confront the Mine Boss of the Baloris Prime system. Use standard tactics against this boss.

After bashing the boss, ascend back up through the levels until you reach the second red door. (With any luck, it will most likely be the first one you hit after rising up from the lower levels). Follow the curving corridor past the door and make for the door at the end. Open this door, then open the one directly opposite it. Keep heading down until you reach another door, open it, and descend into a triangle room. Move to the base of the triangle room, hug the floor then circle down and around to the exit on the other side of the room.

Mine 21—The N'neri Ring

Welcome to the N'neri Ring, the first mission in the Puuma Sphere System. Two new robots appear on this level: The Green Dragon and the Spider, of which the latter spawns off into many smaller robots when killed. Both complicate your mission in the N'neri Ring.

Descend to the floor of the chamber where you start and take the tunnel to the bottommost door. On the right as you enter, you'll see the Guidebot's cage.

Whether you free the Guidebot or not, turn 180 degrees away from the Guidebot cage and head for the tunnel at the other end of the room. Go down the tunnel and take the shaft up. Pass the first level (you'll know it by the robot generator along one wall) and bear to the left, heading up the second shaft you see and stop at the top. Fly over the shallow pit in this room and make your way to the door on the opposite side. Open the door, head down the steel grate corridor to the door at the opposite end. Open it, then bear to the left and down. Circle the hexagonal pillar and pick up the blue key.

Go up and out, back the way you came through the steel grate corridor, back over the room with the shallow pit. Go down the shaft and this

Mine 21 — Level 1

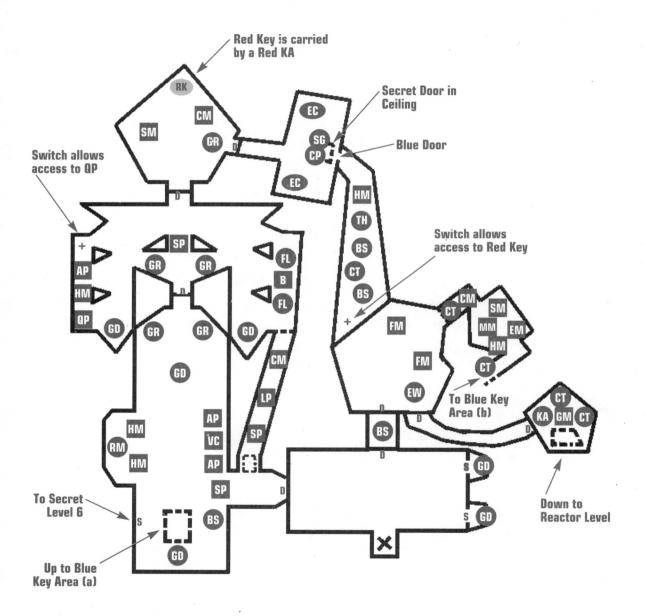

Red Key is carried by a Red KA

Secret Door in Ceiling

Blue Door

Switch allows access to QP

Switch allows access to Red Key

To Blue Key Area (b)

Down to Reactor Level

To Secret Level 6

Up to Blue Key Area (a)

PART 2   Mission Maps

Mine 21—Blue Key Area

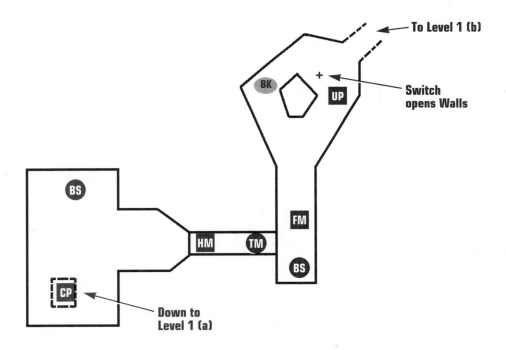

To Level 1 (b)

Switch
opens Walls

Down to
Level 1 (a)

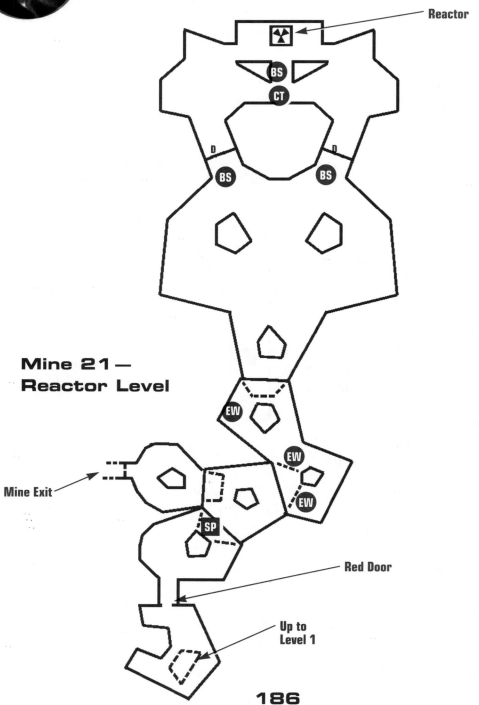

Reactor

BS

CT

D   D

BS   BS

Mine 21—
Reactor Level

EW

EW

Mine Exit

EW

SP

Red Door

Up to
Level 1

time, stop at the level with the robot generator. Fly into the room, then head up to its second level and head out the door.

Directly ahead of you some distance away down a corridor is a door. Fly to it, open it, and go into the room beyond it (it also has a hexagonal pillar running through its center). Descend one level, find a door. Open it, then head for the blue door that lies directly beyond it. Open the blue door and explore the room beyond it for a red Kamikaze robot that is carrying the red key. Destroy it (or let it hurl itself at you), and then take the key.

Exit through the blue door, then go through the door opposite it across the room. Once in the hexagonal room, ascend one level and exit through the door at the top. Shoot straight through the corridor behind the door, making a beeline for the door at the other end. Once there, drop down to the level where the robot generator is. Descend the shaft in that room until you are back in the room where the Guidebot was imprisoned. Take the door out to the large green chamber where you began the level, then head out through the door up on the wall to the left (it is the door opposite your starting position). Open the second door that appears immediately after it, enter the hexagonal room beyond, then descend one level and open the door directly beneath the one you entered. Proceed down the passage to another door and open that one. You will find yourself in *another* hexagonal room. Descend through the hole in the floor.

You will enter another hexagonal room, except this one has a red door. Open the door, then hug the left wall until you reach the energy recharging room. Look for a grate closing off one of the top corners of the room and precision shoot to blow up the panel beyond it and open the grate. This will allow you free access to the exit door once you destroy the reactor (be sure to wipe out any robots guarding it, just for good measure). Once the exit is unobstructed, hug the wall to the right of the exit and follow it around to reach the end room just before the reactor (it will have two doors at the end and three hexagonal pillars supporting it). Head in through one of the doors and blow up the reactor.

After blowing up the reactor, orient yourself so your back is to it, then follow the right hand passage out. Leave via the door, then hug the right wall all the way around until you reach the mine exit.

Mine 22—Kwod A'Rior

Proceed from the insertion point down the corridor. Follow the left-hand wall around the corner to a shaft. Continue down that shaft in the floor. Take the closest shaft down (it will also be the steepest descent). This will lead to a large room with the blue key in an alcove. Take the key and ascend back up the shaft to Level 1 of the mine.

Once you have ascended the shaft move out of the alcove and turn left. Follow the right-hand wall around the corner to another shaft. Descend down the shaft to the blue door at the bottom of the shaft. Enter the blue door and keep to the right-hand wall as you fight your way into the heavily defended level. There will be a trench-like corridor that opens up in both directions as you exit the area near the blue door. Take this corridor to the right. A short distance along the corridor there will be a shaft in the floor leading down. Take this shaft down.

The shaft will slope down towards level 4. Keep a wary eye near the ceiling to forestall a surprise attack from above. This sloping corridor will lead out into a very large room.

Continue straight across the room to a door in the floor of the wall opposite the one that you entered the room from. As you enter the door the vertical shaft up to the yellow key is on your right and an energy center (should you need a refill) is behind a door to your left. Bear to your right as you enter and look for the vertical shaft in the mine ceiling (to the yellow key level). Ascend the shaft and follow the corridor around to the right and then down into the yellow key area. As you ascended the shaft you should have noticed the mine exit in the roof at the top of the mine. Don't forget where that is. You'll need to know it soon enough.

Once you have the yellow key, retrace your steps to the blue door. Ascend the shaft above the blue door back up to Level 1. Follow the corridor around to the yellow door. Open the yellow door and move in to take possession of your prize.

Take the red key back out of the room (through the yellow door). Retrace your steps back to the blue door at the bottom of the shaft on Level 1. Go through the blue door and retrace your steps to the sloping shaft off to your right. Go back down the sloping shaft.

188

Mine 22—Level 1

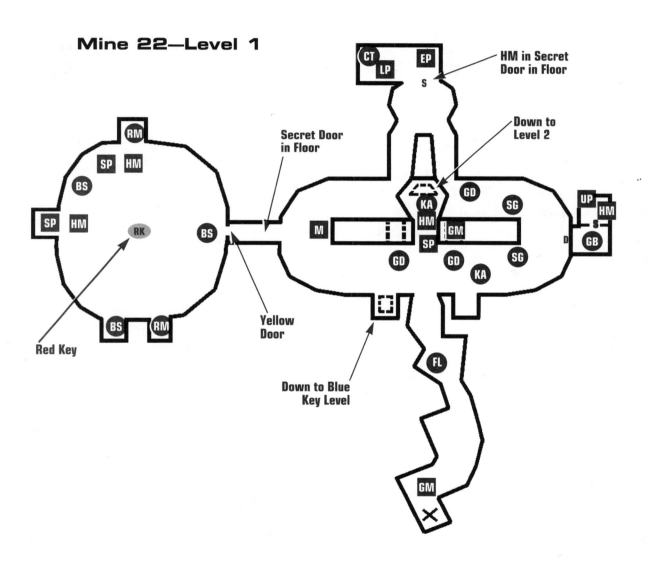

HM in Secret
Door in Floor

Secret Door
in Floor

Down to
Level 2

Red Key

Yellow
Door

Down to Blue
Key Level

Mine 22—Level 2

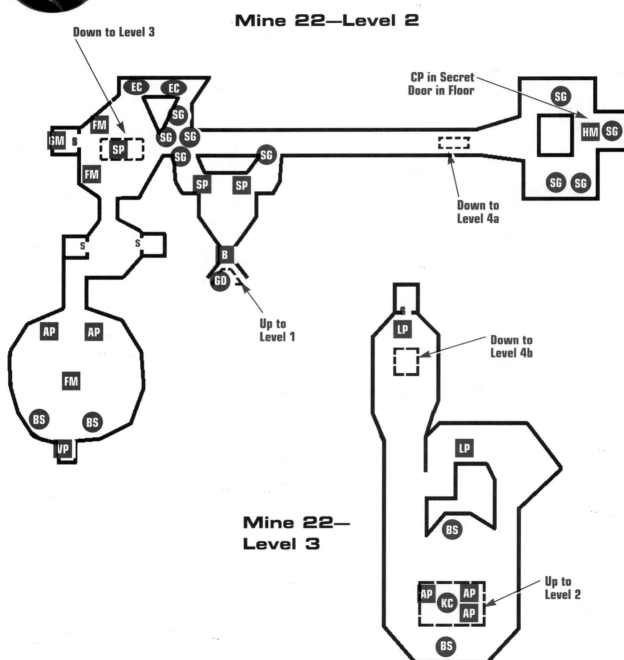

Down to Level 3

EC EC

CP in Secret
Door in Floor

SG

SG

FM

SG

HM SG

GM S

SP

SG SG

SG

SG

FM

SP SP

Down to
Level 4a

SG SG

B

GD

Up to
Level 1

S   S

S

LP

Down to
Level 4b

AP   AP

FM

LP

BS   BS

VP

Mine 22—
Level 3

BS

AP AP
KC
AP

Up to
Level 2

BS

Mine 22—Level 4

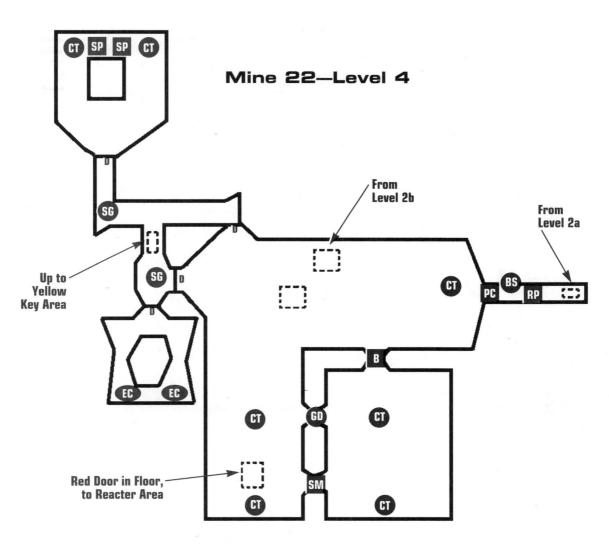

From
Level 2b

From
Level 2a

Up to
Yellow
Key Area

Red Door in Floor,
to Reacter Area

Mine 22—Yellow Key Area

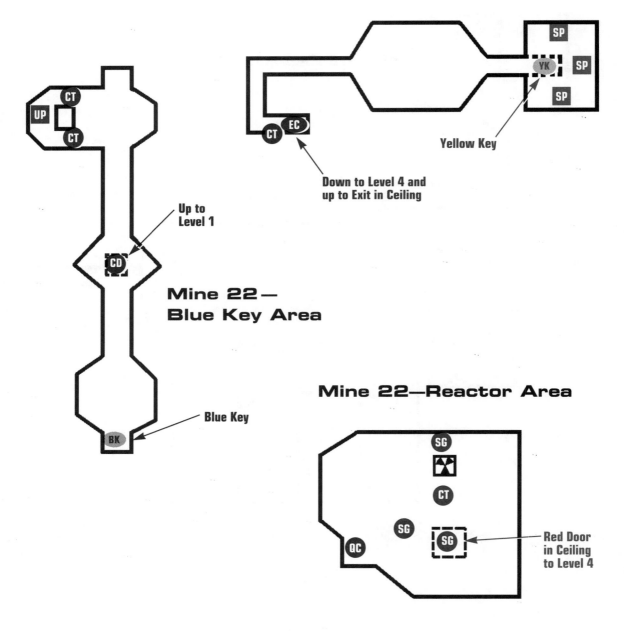

Yellow Key

Down to Level 4 and
up to Exit in Ceiling

Up to
Level 1

Mine 22—
Blue Key Area

Blue Key

Mine 22—Reactor Area

Red Door
in Ceiling
to Level 4

Once you have reentered the large room follow the wall around to the left. Once around the corner you should be able to see a red door in the floor. Enter this door to gain access to the reactor beneath. Come in shooting.

After destroying the reactor retrace your steps back to the shaft that you take to get to the yellow key level. The mine exit is in the very top-most part of the shaft. Fly your way out of the mine before it melts into a radioactive pile of slag.

Mine 23 — Iwihml

Use the door in front of you to exit the room that you start in. Once you leave the room, immediately turn around and go back into the room. A switch will have been revealed in the back left corner. Shoot the switch and leave the room again.

As you pass through the door you will see another door directly across a chasm. If you wish to get the Guidebot you may do so on your way to this door (the Guidebot is imprisoned directly below the wall of the chasm closest to you). Fly across the gap as quickly as possible to avoid hostile fire.

The door that you enter will be at the bottom of a vertical shaft. Climb to the top of the shaft and down into the very next shaft in front of you. The bottom of that next shaft will contain the blue key.

From the shaft containing the blue key travel upwards and forward towards the blue door in the ceiling of the shaft in front of you. Enter that door to retrieve the yellow key.

Go back to the door labeled 'To level 1(b)' on your map. Proceed through this door. Turn to the right and follow the wall all the way around the corner to the yellow door. This door should be on your right hand side as you approach it. Proceed through the yellow door and into the red key area to retrieve the red key.

Leave the room and stick to the left wall as you exit. This route will take you out the same way you came in. Continue to follow the left wall

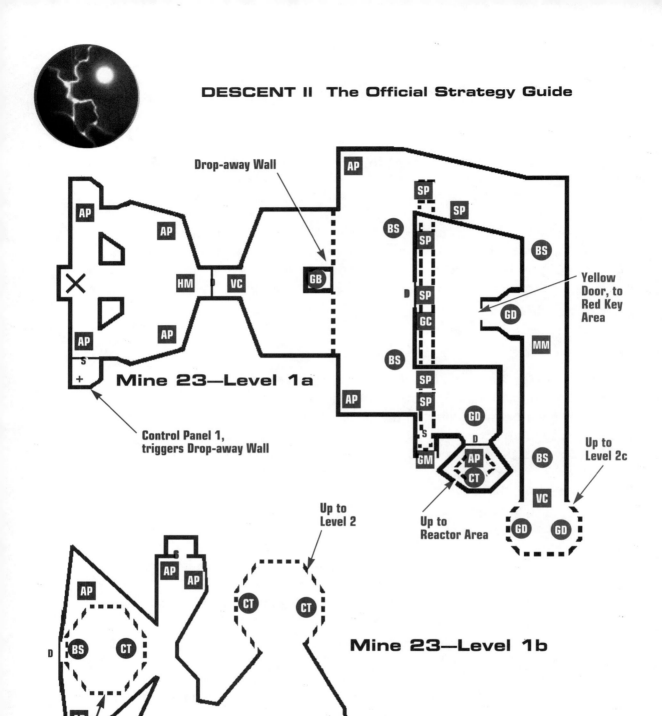

Drop-away Wall

AP

SP

SP

BS

SP

BS

Yellow Door, to Red Key Area

HM VC GB

D

SP

GC

GD

BS

MM

Mine 23—Level 1a

AP

BS

SP

SP

AP

S

GD

Control Panel 1, triggers Drop-away Wall

D

GM

AP

CT

BS

Up to Reactor Area

VC

Up to Level 2c

GD GD

Up to Level 2

S

AP AP

CT CT

AP

Mine 23—Level 1b

D BS CT

AP

Up to Level 2

Mine 23—Level 2

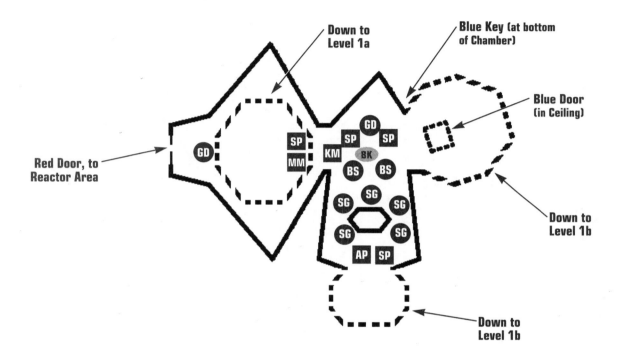

Down to
Level 1a

Blue Key (at bottom
of Chamber)

Blue Door
(in Ceiling)

Red Door, to
Reactor Area

Down to
Level 1b

Down to
Level 1b

Mine 23—Yellow Key Area

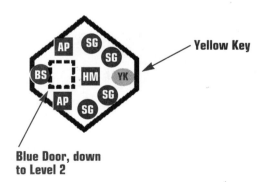

Yellow Key

Blue Door, down
to Level 2

Mine 23—Red Key Area

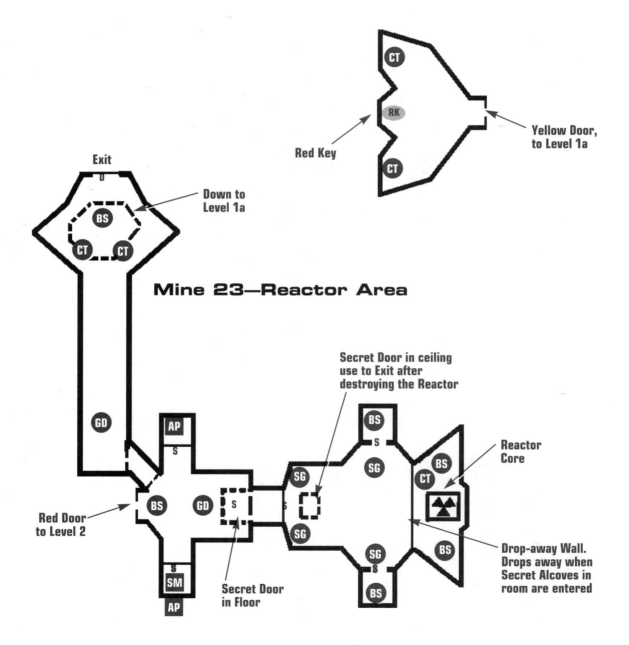

Red Key

Yellow Door, to Level 1a

Exit

Down to Level 1a

Mine 23—Reactor Area

Secret Door in ceiling use to Exit after destroying the Reactor

Reactor Core

Red Door to Level 2

Secret Door in Floor

Drop-away Wall. Drops away when Secret Alcoves in room are entered all the way around sticking to the bottom of the chasm this time. Proceed through the door on your map that reads 'Up to Reactor Level.'

This door will open into the bottom of a vertical shaft. Take the shaft all they way up to the top. At the top of the shaft there will be a corridor leading away from the shaft and the mine exit will be directly opposite this corridor. Make note of the mine exit.

Proceed down the corridor to the red door. As you enter you will be attacked by robots guarding the entrance to the Reactor. Destroy all the robots in the room—it will make your next task that much easier. After destroying all the robots open one of the two red doors in the room. This will open two secret doors into the room. You must enter both of the areas revealed by the opening of the secret doors. Once you have done that, a secret door will open in the floor of the main room. Go through this door in the floor of the main room. This will lead you into the room just before the reactor. As you approach the reactor (currently concealed by a wall) secret alcoves on either side of the room will open. Destroy the robots freed by this and enter both secret alcoves. Trigger any switches that you see. This will drop the wall concealing the reactor.

Destroy the reactor and leave by the secret door that has just opened in the ceiling of the room. This will take you back into the room with the red doors. Take the bottom one back to the tunnel that you took to enter this area. Remember that mine exit we noticed on the way in? Take that out of the mine.

Mine 24—Tycho Brahe

From your insertion point you will see a red door directly across from you. Directly above this red door is the mine exit. It's always a good idea to know where the door out is.

Move forward to the red door. Turn towards your right and follow the curving corridor around until your path is blocked. At the end of this segment there is a Centurion hiding around the corner. Also, Kamikaze mine-layers will harass you. Do not be sidetracked too much in an attempt to catch these mine-laying pests.

When you get to the end of the corridor you will have a choice of going either up or down. You want to go up as the entrance to the blue key area is through a normal door at the top of this loop.

As you enter the blue key area make note of the blue door just outside.

The blue key area is a two-tiered room. By sticking to the side walls of the room as you enter you will be able to rise all the way to the upper room. The blue key is in an alcove in this upper level.

When you take the key a force field will block your exit. The roof above the key will open, though, allowing you access to a quad laser powerup and a switch that will turn off the force field.

As you leave the room in which you found the blue key you will see the blue door just below the regular door through which you entered this area. Dive down through this blue door to find the yellow key at the bottom of a well defended room.

Continue out of the blue door and as you exit through the blue door turn around so that you are facing the blue door from the outside. The regular door should now be to your right. Proceed straight ahead. Turn right and follow the curvature of the mine down to the next corridor intersection. At that intersection turn left and follow that corridor until you get to the energy center. Replenish your energy here. As soon as you replenish your energy you will be able to find the yellow door on the opposite wall of the corridor.

Enter that yellow door. As you enter the room you will see the red door directly across from you. The red key is at the bottom of the room. You will have to fire through the grate separating you from the red key in order to hit a wall switch that allows access to the red key.

Take the red key and enter the end Boss level through the red door in the same room.

This Boss is the toughest yet. It is able to fire two shaker missiles at the same time. Even a near miss with a shaker missile is enough to destroy your ship, Material Defender. The utmost care and caution must be used here, with special emphasis on caution.

As soon as you have destroyed the Mine Boss an external view of your escape will be shown. Sit back and enjoy the ride, Material Defender, you have done well.

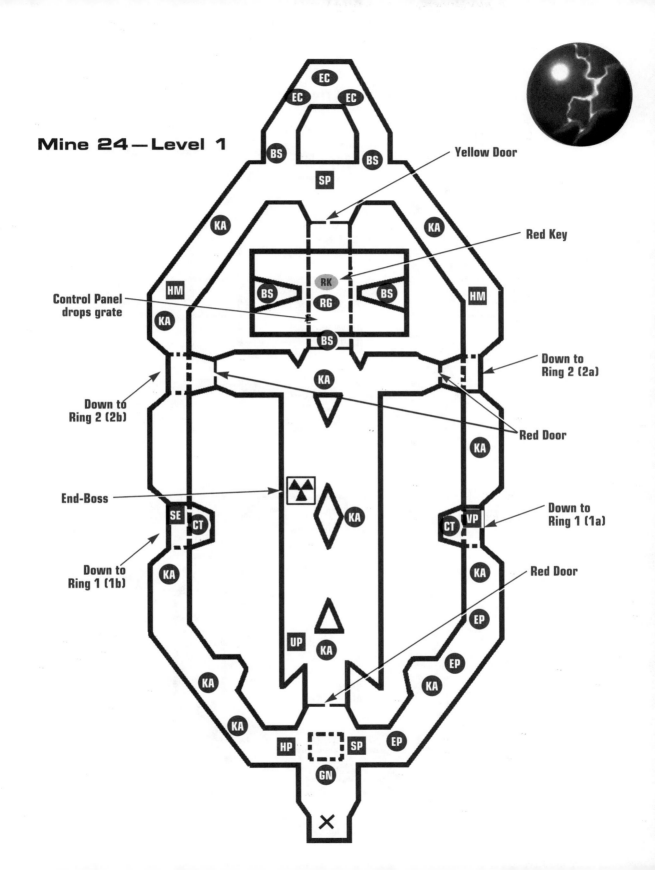

Mine 24 – Level 1

Yellow Door

Red Key

Control Panel drops grate

Down to Ring 2 (2a)

Red Door

Down to Ring 2 (2b)

End-Boss

Down to Ring 1 (1a)

Down to Ring 1 (1b)

Red Door

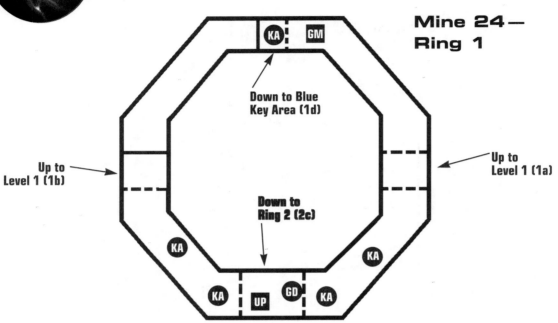

**Mine 24 —
Ring 1**

Down to Blue
Key Area (1d)

Up to
Level 1 (1b)

Up to
Level 1 (1a)

Down to
Ring 2 (2c)

KA GM

KA

KA

KA UP GD KA

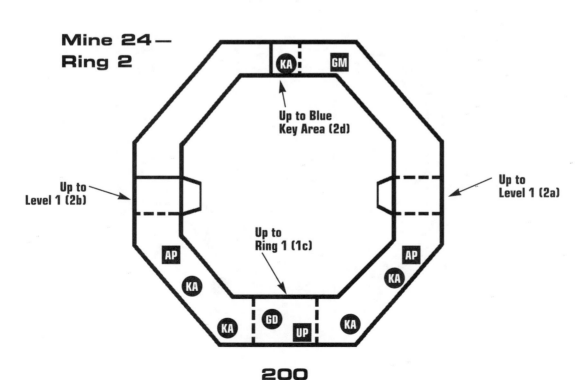

**Mine 24 —
Ring 2**

Up to Blue
Key Area (2d)

Up to
Level 1 (2b)

Up to
Level 1 (2a)

Up to
Ring 1 (1c)

KA GM

AP

AP

KA

KA

KA GD UP KA

Mine 24—Blue Key Area

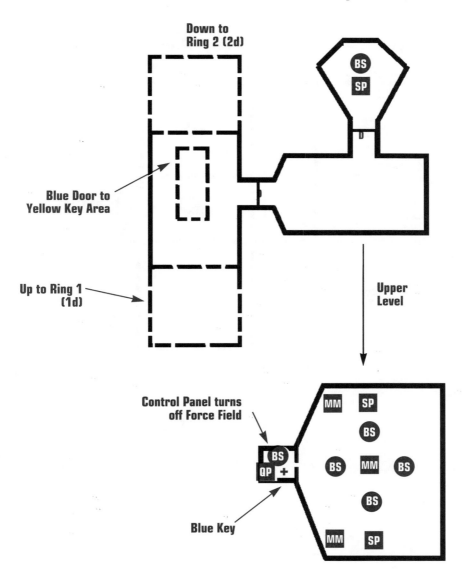

Mine 24—Yellow Key Area

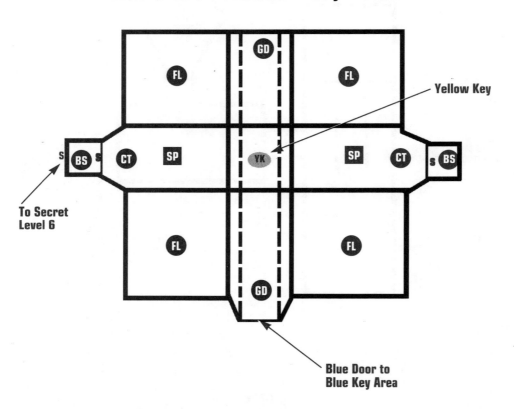

PART 3

SECRET LEVELS

Secret Level 1—Segment City

It's enough to warp your mind. This level is full of one-way hallways and doors, not to mention a plethora of control panel switches to play with. Can you figure out how to navigate this mine without trapping yourself?

Secret Level 2—Hurdle Chase

This beautiful underground grotto would be a treat to any miner. Unfortunately, it is now patrolled by Salamander robots whose sole purpose is to keep intruders out by constantly patrolling and mining the area.

Secret Level 3—Mephisto Hardcore

You have stumbled across one of the alien robots' main thermal energy centers. Right now it is under construction. When complete, this center alone could power thousands of alien robots for decades. It's your job to take this center out before it is fully functional.

Secret Level 4—Galacia Caverns

You must save the hostages at all cost, but the only way to accomplish this is to destroy the reactor core so as to short out the door keeping you trapped in the reactor room. It's going to be close, but it can be done.

Secret Level 5—Ascent Level 1

The alien robots are better prepared this time. They've managed to build a shield around the reactor core. Figure out how to lower the shielding, destroy the reactor and escape the mine.

Secret Level 6—Chain Reaction

This seems to be a new kind of reactor you haven't seen before. Somehow the alien robots have been able to interconnect multiple reactor cores. Find and destroy all reactors before time runs out.

Secret Level 1 — Level 1

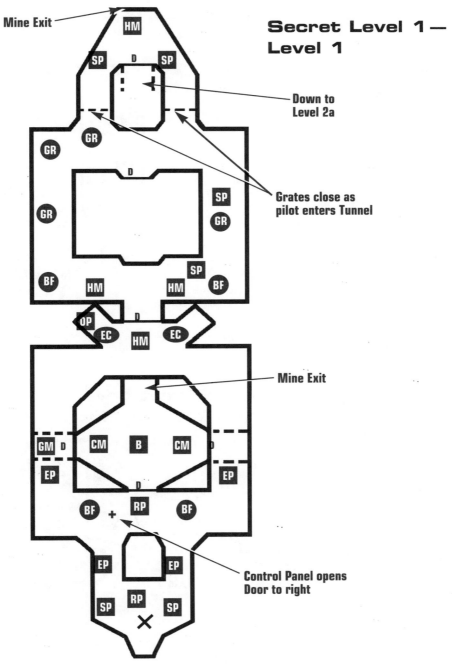

Mine Exit

Down to Level 2a

Grates close as pilot enters Tunnel

Mine Exit

Control Panel opens Door to right

Secret Level 1—Level 2a

Secret Level 1— Level 2b

Secret Level 1— Reactor Room

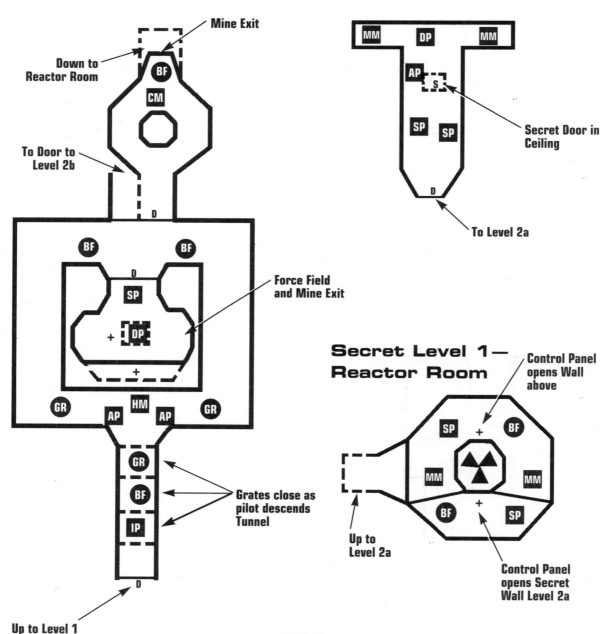

Mine Exit

Down to Reactor Room

To Door to Level 2b

Force Field and Mine Exit

Grates close as pilot descends Tunnel

Up to Level 1

Secret Door in Ceiling

To Level 2a

Control Panel opens Wall above

Up to Level 2a

Control Panel opens Secret Wall Level 2a

PART 3   Secret Levels

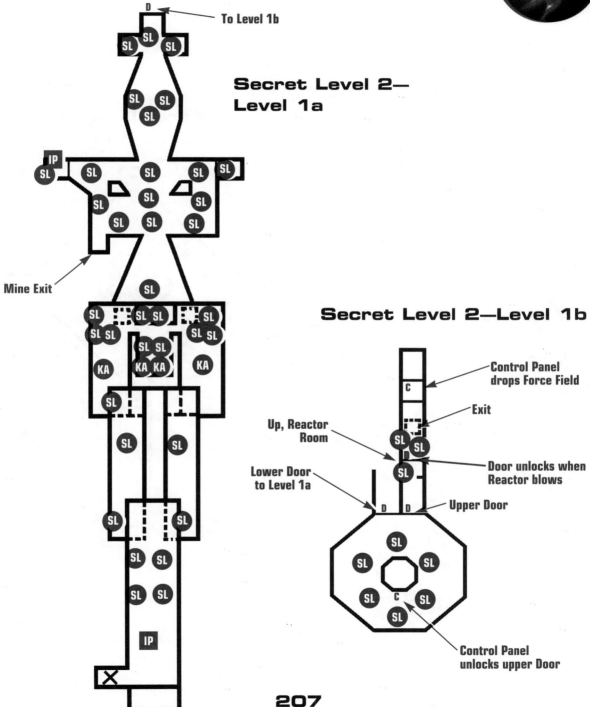

To Level 1b

Secret Level 2—
Level 1a

Mine Exit

Secret Level 2—Level 1b

Control Panel drops Force Field

Exit

Up, Reactor Room

Door unlocks when Reactor blows

Lower Door to Level 1a

Upper Door

Control Panel unlocks upper Door

207

DESCENT II The Official Strategy Guide

Secret Level 2—Reactor Room

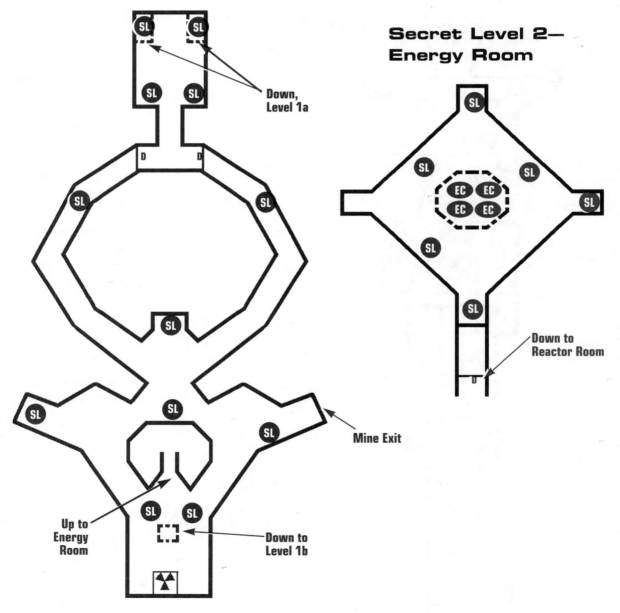

Secret Level 2—
Energy Room

Down,
Level 1a

Down to
Reactor Room

Mine Exit

Up to
Energy
Room

Down to
Level 1b

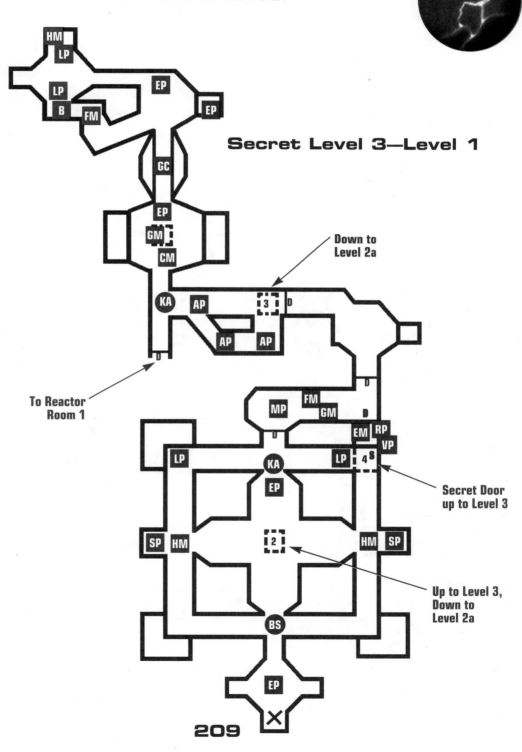

PART 3   Secret Levels

Secret Level 3—Level 1

Down to
Level 2a

To Reactor
Room 1

Secret Door
up to Level 3

Up to Level 3,
Down to
Level 2a

209

Secret Level 3— Level 2b

Secret Level 3—Level 2a

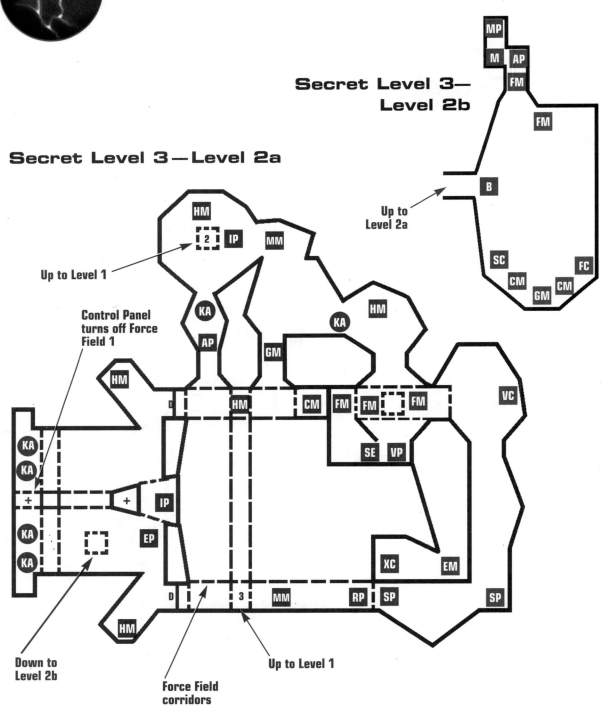

Up to Level 2a

Up to Level 1

Control Panel turns off Force Field 1

Down to Level 2b

Force Field corridors

Up to Level 1

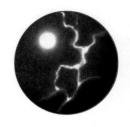

Secret Level 3—Level 3

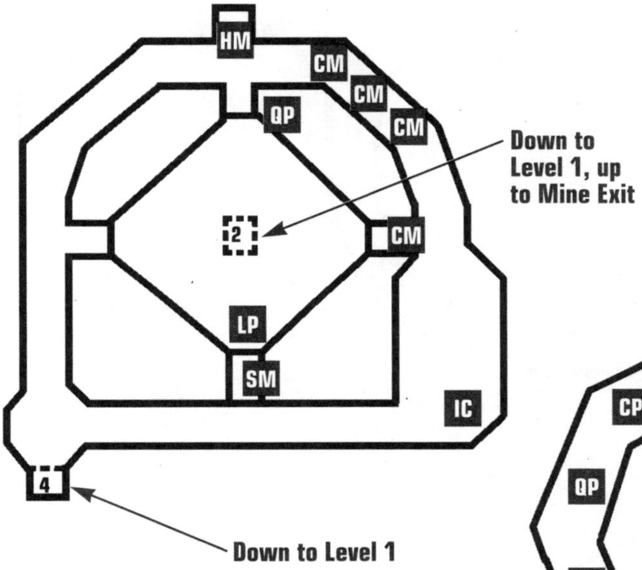
HM
CM
CM
CM
QP
Down to Level 1, up to Mine Exit
2
CM
LP
SM
IC
4
Down to Level 1

Secret Level 3—Reactor Room 1

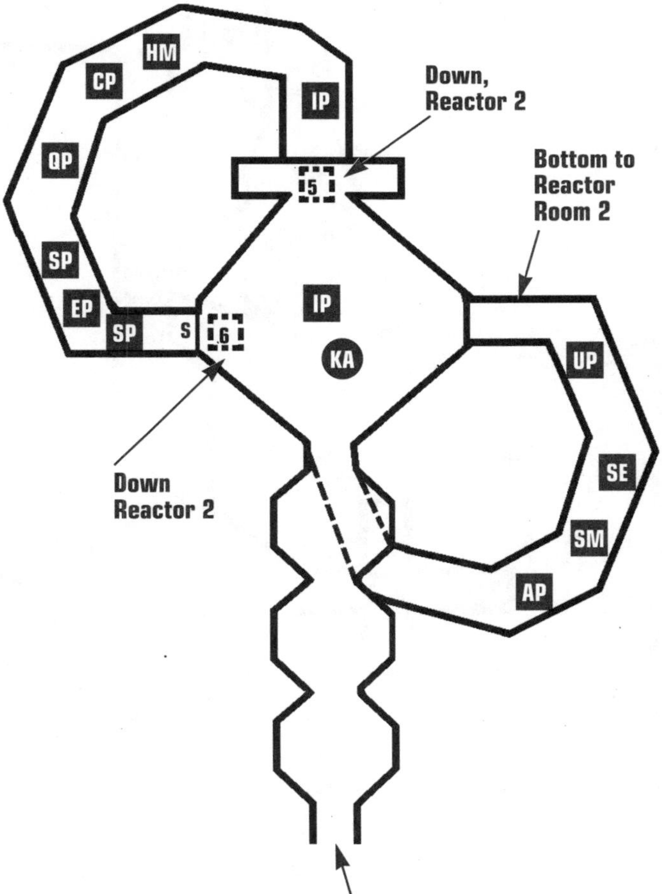
HM
CP
IP
Down, Reactor 2
QP
5
Bottom to Reactor Room 2
SP
IP
EP
SP
S
6
KA
UP
Down Reactor 2
SE
SM
AP
To Level 1

Secret Level 3—Reactor Room 2

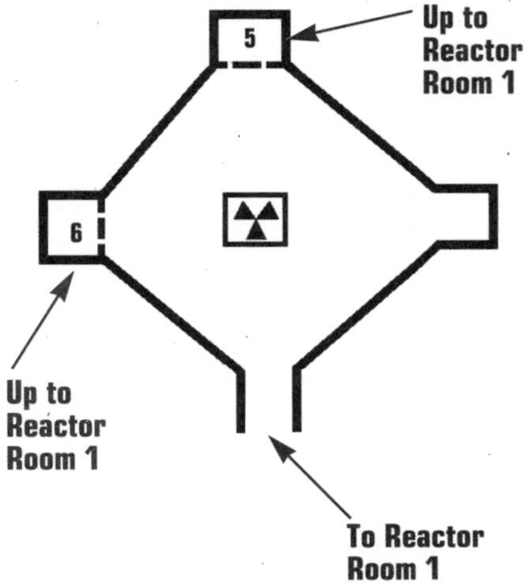
5
Up to Reactor Room 1
6
Up to Reactor Room 1
To Reactor Room 1

Secret Level 4 —
Level 1a

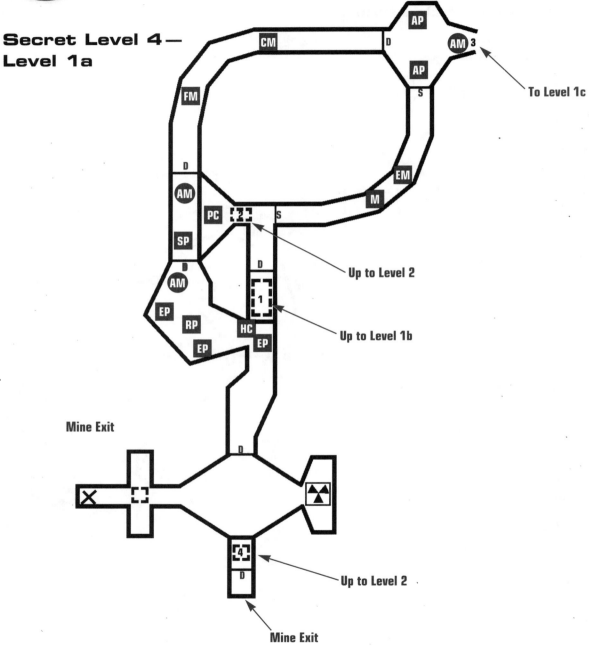

To Level 1c

Up to Level 2

Up to Level 1b

Mine Exit

Up to Level 2

Mine Exit

PART 3   Secret Levels

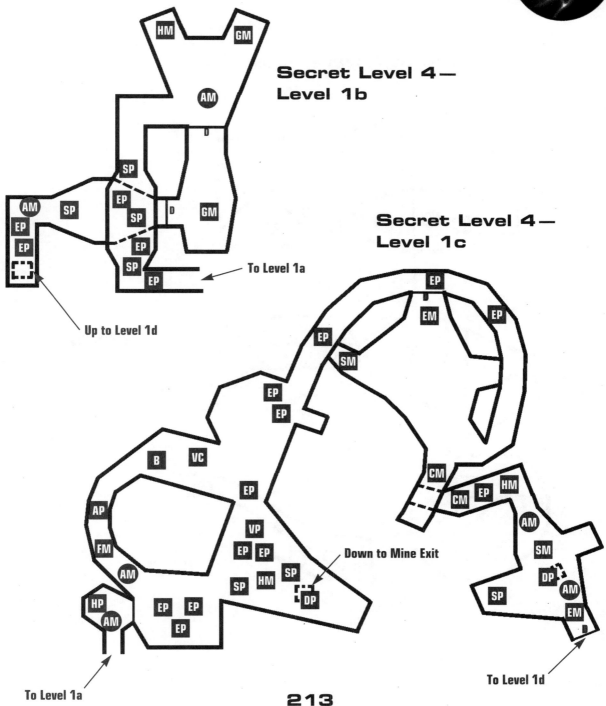

Secret Level 4—
Level 1b

Secret Level 4—
Level 1c

To Level 1a

Up to Level 1d

Down to Mine Exit

To Level 1a

To Level 1d

DESCENT II The Official Strategy Guide

Secret Level 4—Level 1d

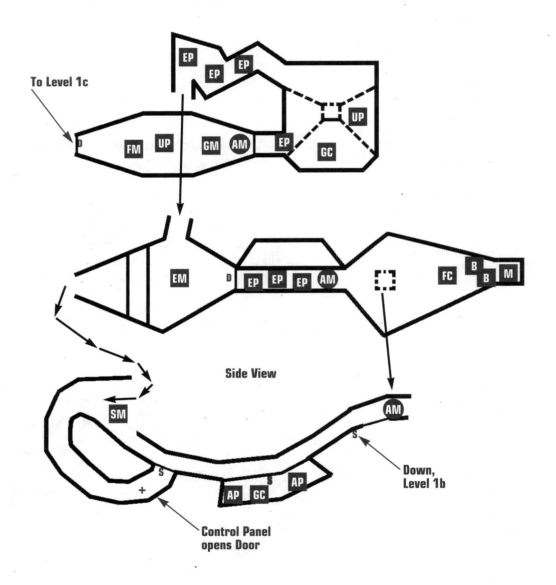

To Level 1c

Side View

SM

AM

S

Down,
Level 1b

AP GC AP

S

+

Control Panel
opens Door

Secret Level 4—Level 2

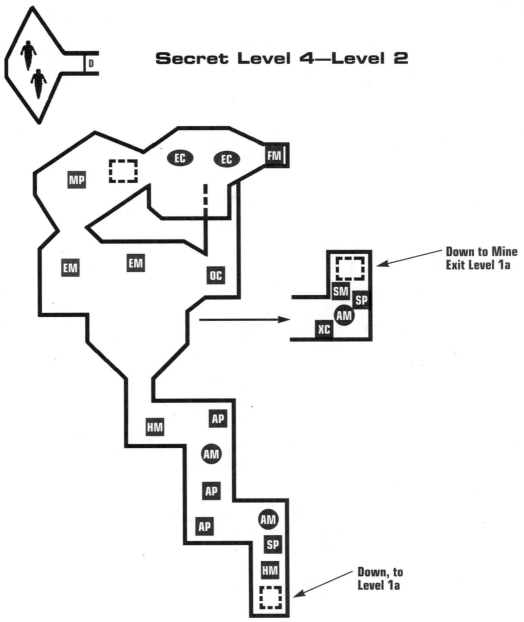

Down to Mine
Exit Level 1a

Down, to
Level 1a

215

Secret Level 5—Level 1

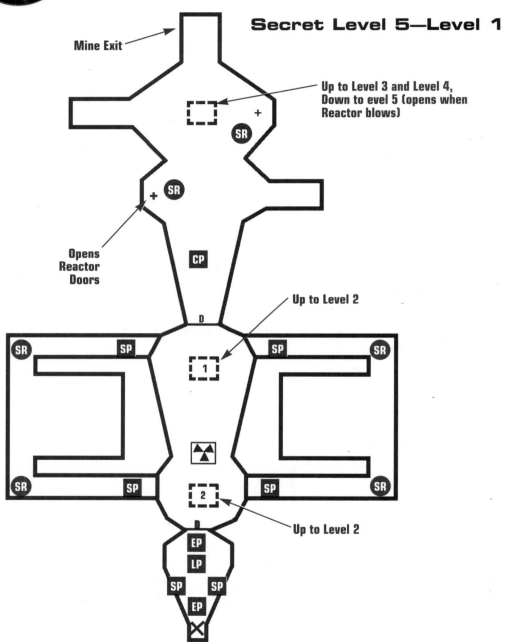

Mine Exit

Up to Level 3 and Level 4,
Down to evel 5 (opens when
Reactor blows)

SR

+ SR

Opens
Reactor
Doors

CP

Up to Level 2

D

SR   SP   SP   SR

1

SP   SP

SR   SP   SP   SR

2

Up to Level 2

EP
LP
SP   SP
EP

Secret Level 5—Level 2

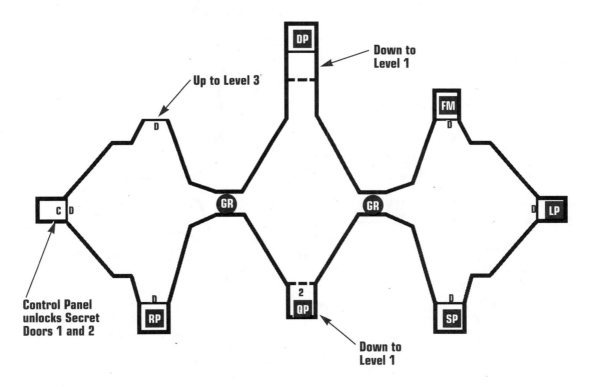

Down to
Level 1

Up to Level 3

Control Panel
unlocks Secret
Doors 1 and 2

Down to
Level 1

Secret Level 5—Level 3

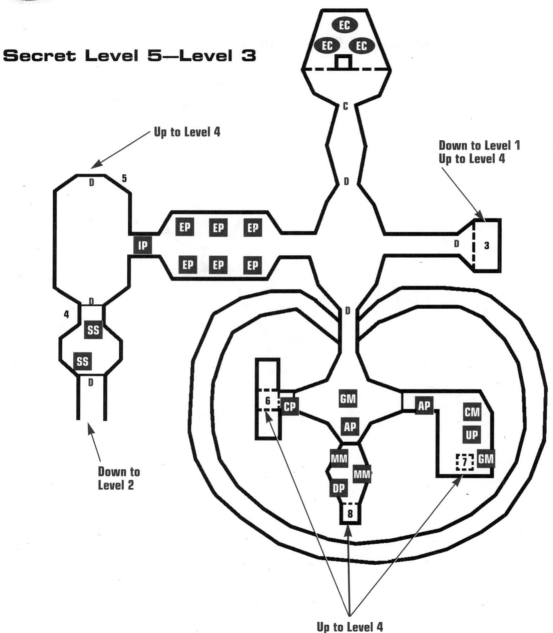

Up to Level 4

Down to Level 1
Up to Level 4

Down to
Level 2

Up to Level 4

Secret Level 5—Level 4

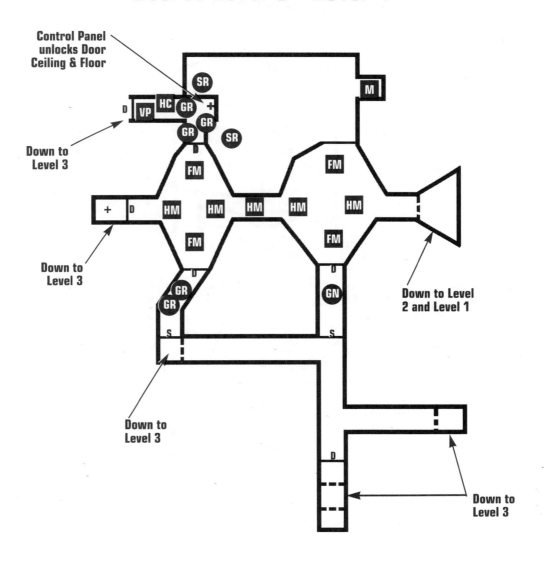

Control Panel
unlocks Door
Ceiling & Floor

Down to
Level 3

Down to
Level 3

Down to
Level 3

Down to Level
2 and Level 1

Down to
Level 3

Secret Level 5—Level 5

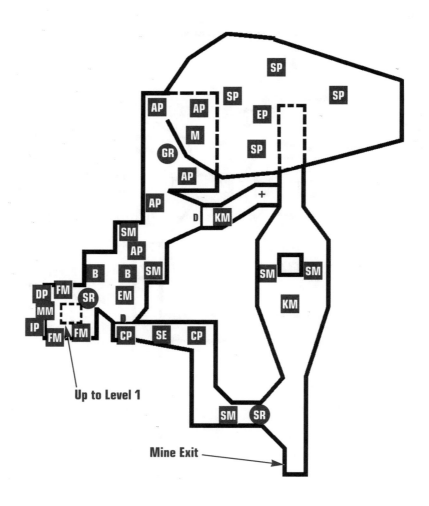

Up to Level 1

Mine Exit

Secret Level 6—Level 1

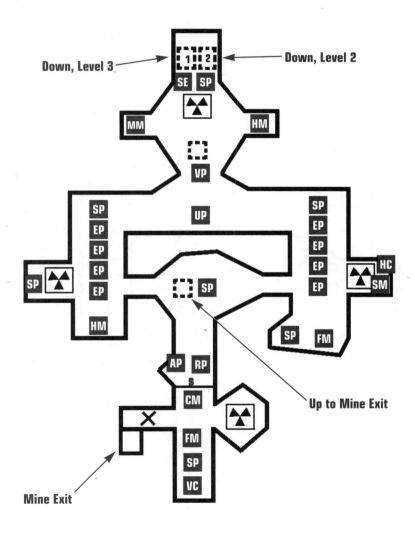

Down, Level 3

Down, Level 2

Up to Mine Exit

Mine Exit

Secret Level 6—Level 2

Secret Level 6—Level 3

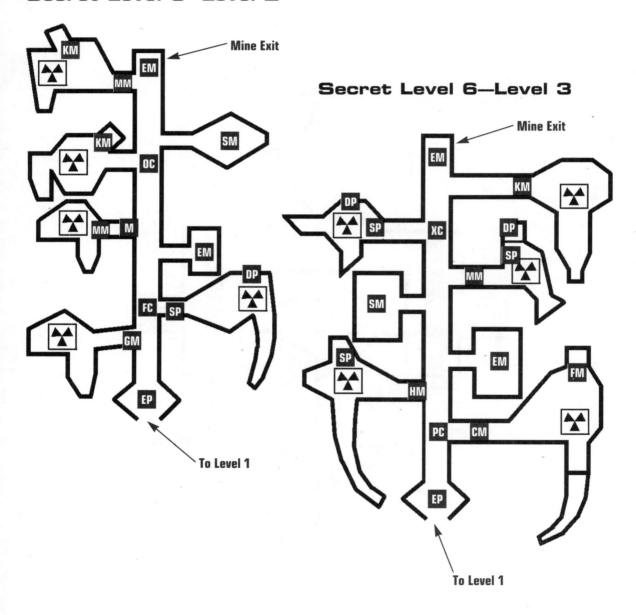

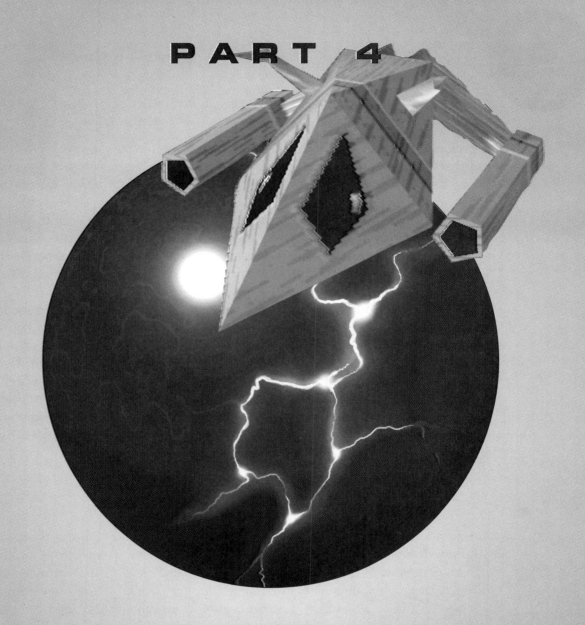

PART 4

MULTIPLAYER
DESCENT II

Tips to Live and Fight By

Descent II offers a dynamic, fully-3D environment where pilots have full control of their ship in six degrees of movement. One can rotate around three different axes, or move in three different directions, or do all of these at the same time. There is no absolute up, down, or sideways, just whatever the circumstances demand. In solo-play, enemy robots maliciously take advantage of this fact in their efforts to destroy you—robots will swarm a pilot from all directions, and one will retreat into a drop-shaft in the ceiling, waiting until you've dealt with the others and turned your back on him before striking. The true 3D environment of *Descent II*, coupled with the robots' abilities and sophisticated artificial intelligence, forces the pilot to adapt and think in three dimensions in order to complete a successful mission—if not to simply stay alive.

Yet, despite all the skills a player develops to become successful at solo play, they are not enough when the opponents cease to be computer-controlled robots. Playing with other human players is like adding another dimension to the list of three that are already incorporated into the game. For this reason, new strategies, tactics, and skills must be developed by the player in order to become successful in multiplayer games.

Fundamental Skills

The first skills to learn are the fundamental ones and chief among these is strafing. This already is a skill that is important to solo play, but in multiplayer games, it is crucial. The basic idea behind strafing is to provide a difficult target by remaining in constant motion, while at the same time keeping the nose of your ship pointed at your opponent. This idea can be condensed down to: Move in one direction, fire in another.

The mechanics of strafing are a little more involved, but become second nature with practice. Think about creating a control setup that allows flexibility and feels natural. Many players opt for a joystick with a hat, others prefer a combination of joystick and keyboard, still others do away with joysticks entirely and just use a mouse and keyboard. The devices are unimportant, what *is* important is that you, the player, can slide in three dimensions naturally and without having to give the process a second thought.

One valuable tactic to use with strafing is to slide vertically while firing. This is effective because most players don't think enough about the vertical dimension. Most dogfights in a large room resolve themselves into a turning war where pilots slide around in a large circle, each trying to out-turn his opponent and get the kill. If you find yourself in just such an engagement, fly around for perhaps a couple of revolutions until you have a good sense of your opponent's intended path, then slide down underneath while keeping your weapons trained on him and open fire as soon as you have a good angle. This unexpected maneuver catches most pilots by surprise and buys you a little time while he tries to compensate. It takes some practice, but when you become proficient with it, you will soon be receiving not just other pilots' curses, but their respect as well.

Once you feel comfortable with strafing in three dimensions, learn how to lead a target. Strafing and leading a target effectively are the two most important skills of every good pilot. Leading involves aiming your weapons along your opponent's line of movement and a short length in front of him, thereby offsetting the time it takes your weapons fire to travel the distance between the two of you. Each weapon you use has unique characteristics and requires a different lead angle, so it is important to learn the nuances of each weapon. Some weapons like the fusion cannon and concussion missiles travel at a relatively slow velocity and require a large lead angle; others, like the Phoenix Cannon are faster and require a smaller lead angle. Whichever weapon you use, learn its characteristics and how to lead a moving target with it.

Another fundamental skill is the ability to use the geometry of your environment to your advantage. Hiding in a shadowed corner in a room makes for an effective ambush, or knowing where the powerups are more likely to regenerate can mean the difference between success and failure. The key point is to know the level where a battle takes place intimately. By doings so, you will know where best to fight and what tactics to employ.

Another aspect of multiplayer fighting that is not normally considered is clutter. When two opponents face each other off in a dogfight and both have rapid fire weapons, the amount of individual shots on the screen at any one particular moment can be quite high. This sometimes serves to obscure your target behind a wall of laser fire traveling both ways. It is often better and more energy efficient to hold off before firing until you

have the best lead angle and to fire in controlled bursts. In a dark room especially, this will give you the advantage of seeing where your opponent is by the rain of weapons fire coming off his guns, while you fade back against the background.

Conversely, if you find yourself in a defensive position, you may want to try unleashing a continuous stream of primary and secondary weapons. In a bright room, this can sometimes overload a pilot's senses as he tries to sort all the objects on the screen at once, giving you the edge to pull off an effective retreat.

Weapons Use in a Multiplayer Arena

The skills and tactics discussed so far are fairly straightforward in comprehension and execution, what should be considered next involves each of the new weapons and how best to utilize them in a multiplayer arena.

Smart-mines and proximity bombs are not normally considered as an effective offensive weapon, but this is not necessarily true. All you need to convert a mine into an offensive weapon is an enemy pilot who is willing to follow you to hell and back just to score a kill. The only trick is to get them to follow you. One effective way is to only engage an opponent briefly, then fly away. Most pilots, especially those with enough shields and armament, will be happy to oblige. As soon as they start the chase, all that is needed is the proper location to drop the mines. The one cautionary note in this, is that if your pursuer is close enough he will be firing his weapons at you and might detonate a mine as you are dropping it. In this case the explosion from a proximity bomb would damage your shields, and the bomblets of a smart-mine would actually lock on to you instead.

There are also creative uses for smart-mines. Drop a marker just outside a door that is often used by other pilots, then position yourself some distance away on the other side and drop a smart-mine or two right next to the door. What can happen is that an opposing pilot may fly toward the door intending to go through it, but just as he does so you will be able to spot him if you keyed in the marker view into one of your windows. As he fires to open the door, use your weapons to detonate the smart-mines. All the bomblets will lock onto your opponent and hit him before he even has a chance to realize what just happened. This little tactic will not endear you to your friends, but it is effective.

One other creative use for a smart mine is if you happen to be cloaked or are so low on shields that death is imminent, ram an opponent and release a smart-mine simultaneously. If you are cloaked, all of the bomblets will lock onto your opponent, and if you are not cloaked, at least some of the bomblets will lock onto him as well. This isn't a very common tactic, but if executed properly will anger and frustrate your opponent to the point of furious distraction.

The gauss and vulcan cannons can be extremely deadly in the hands of a proficient pilot. Their advantage is that they are instantaneous. This means that they require no lead angle and leave no trail of fire as the shots travel to their target, consequently giving no indication of your position. In a darkened room, the gauss cannon can be devastating. It's knock-back can completely disorient an opponent as he is knocked about, and without a trail of fire giving away your position, it is that much harder for him to spot you.

One less obvious benefit to the gauss and vulcan is that since they require no energy, your energy can actually increase while fighting and scoring kills. Most often an opponent will release an energy boost upon his demise. When you use the vulcan or gauss cannons, your energy will not be depleted and it will only increase with each kill you score. If you also have the energy-shield converter powerup, this translates into an effective means to increase your shields on a regular basis.

The phoenix cannon can be a very deadly weapon in the right hands but requires careful attention to its use. Due to its extremely high rate of fire, the phoenix will inflict a lot of damage to a player before he even realizes he's been hit. Due to the fact that the shots bounce, it is also possible to fire from extreme off-angles and still score a hit. This can be useful in that an opponent will be hit without even realizing from what direction the attack originally came. The ability to fire from around corners can also be effective for setting up traps. By setting a marker in the proper location, you can see a pilot approach and, if you have already tested the right angle, fire off a volley to bounce its way straight towards him. With an intense enough stream, the opposing pilot will not even know what hit him before he's dead. The downside to the use of the phoenix cannon is that

you have to pay very close attention to its bounce or it will otherwise cut down your shields before you even realize you miscalculated your angles.

Of the new missiles offered in *Descent II*, the guided missile offers the most creative potential in a multiplayer game. Its downside is that your ship is left stationary while you are piloting the missile, but if your ship is in a safe position this drawback is negligible. With a guided missile it is possible to position your ship in dark shadows and strike at an opponent without him ever being able to spot your location. Also, it is possible to be in a tunnel outside a chamber where a large firefight is occurring and pick off your opponents one-by-one. A guided missile also provides the opportunity to scout ahead without putting your ship in direct danger.

Miscellaneous Tips

Another item whose offensive use is not immediately apparent is the afterburner. When in the middle of a dogfight with another pilot, let off a large volley of weapons fire just ahead of an opponent. While he is busy attempting to dodge the fire, you can hit the afterburner and end up immediately behind him without him realizing what you have done. The very same maneuver can be used to perform a successful evasion.

Other things to consider are headlights. Although quite useful when delving into the dark areas of a mine, they can be very expensive in a multiplayer engagement. Leaving your Headlights on is a sure way of broadcasting your position to your opponents, and, they also drain valuable energy that could be better used powering your weapons. Make sure you select the headlights to be defaulted off whenever you pick up the powerup.

One tactic when you are extremely low on shields and you know that death is imminent is to eject a weapon or powerup into a secret or obscure location. This will both deny an opponent some of the spoils of war and make it possible for you to easily reacquire a powerful weapon when you regenerate. It may take some practice to eject weapons accurately, but in the long-run the benefits are well worth the trouble.

Computer Game Books

1942: The Pacific Air War—The Official Strategy Guide	$19.95
The 11th Hour: The Official Strategy Guide	$19.95
The 7th Guest: The Official Strategy Guide	$19.95
Aces Over Europe: The Official Strategy Guide	$19.95
Across the Rhine: The Official Strategy Guide	$19.95
Alone in the Dark 3: The Official Strategy Guide	$19.95
Armored Fist: The Official Strategy Guide	$19.95
Ascendancy: The Official Strategy Guide	$19.95
Buried in Time: The Journeyman Project 2— The Official Strategy Guide	$19.95
CD-ROM Games Secrets, Volume 1	$19.95
Caesar II: The Official Strategy Guide	$19.95
Celtic Tales: Balor of the Evil Eye— The Official Strategy Guide	$19.95
Cyberia: The Official Strategy Guide	$19.95
Computer Adventure Games Secrets	$19.95
Dark Seed II: The Official Strategy Guide	$19.95
Descent: The Official Strategy Guide	$19.95
DOOM Battlebook	$19.95
DOOM II: The Official Strategy Guide	$19.95
Dracula Unleashed: The Official Strategy Guide & Novel	$19.95
Dragon Lore: The Official Strategy Guide	$19.95
Dungeon Master II: The Legend of Skullkeep— The Official Strategy Guide	$19.95
Fleet Defender: The Official Strategy Guide	$19.95
Frankenstein: Through the Eyes of the Monster— The Official Strategy Guide	$19.95
Front Page Sports Football Pro '95: The Official Playbook	$19.95
Fury3: The Official Strategy Guide	$19.95
Hell: A Cyberpunk Thriller— The Official Strategy Guide	$19.95
Heretic: The Official Strategy Guide	$19.95
I Have No Mouth, and I Must Scream: The Official Strategy Guide	$19.95
In The 1st Degree: The Official Strategy Guide	$19.95
Kingdom: The Far Reaches— The Official Strategy Guide	$14.95
King's Quest VII: The Unauthorized Strategy Guide	$19.95
The Legend of Kyrandia: The Official Strategy Guide	$19.95
Lords of Midnight: The Official Strategy Guide	$19.95
Machiavelli the Prince: Official Secrets & Solutions	$12.95
Marathon: The Official Strategy Guide	$19.95
Master of Orion: The Official Strategy Guide	$19.95
Master of Magic: The Official Strategy Guide	$19.95
Microsoft Arcade: The Official Strategy Guide	$12.95
Microsoft Flight Simulator 5.1: The Official Strategy Guide	$19.95
Microsoft Golf: The Official Strategy Guide	$19.95

Microsoft Space Simulator: The Official Strategy Guide	$19.95
Might and Magic Compendium: The Authorized Strategy Guide for Games I, II, III, and IV	$19.95
Myst: The Official Strategy Guide	$19.95
Online Games: In-Depth Strategies and Secrets	$19.95
Oregon Trail II: The Official Strategy Guide	$19.95
The Pagemaster: Official CD-ROM Strategy Guide	$14.95
Panzer General: The Official Strategy Guide	$19.95
Perfect General II: The Official Strategy Guide	$19.95
Prince of Persia: The Official Strategy Guide	$19.95
Prisoner of Ice: The Official Strategy Guide	$19.95
Rebel Assault: The Official Insider's Guide	$19.95
The Residents: Bad Day on the Midway— The Official Strategy Guide	$19.95
Return to Zork Adventurer's Guide	$14.95
Romance of the Three Kingdoms IV: Wall of Fire—The Official Strategy Guide	$19.95
Shadow of the Comet: The Official Strategy Guide	$19.95
Shannara: The Official Strategy Guide	$19.95
Sid Meier's Civilization, or Rome on 640K a Day	$19.95
Sid Meier's Colonization: The Official Strategy Guide	$19.95
SimCity 2000: Power, Politics, and Planning	$19.95
SimEarth: The Official Strategy Guide	$19.95
SimFarm Almanac: The Official Guide to SimFarm	$19.95
SimLife: The Official Strategy Guide	$19.95
SimTower: The Official Strategy Guide	$19.95
Stonekeep: The Official Strategy Guide	$19.95
SubWar 2050: The Official Strategy Guide	$19.95
Terry Pratchett's Discworld: The Official Strategy Guide	$19.95
TIE Fighter: The Official Strategy Guide	$19.95
TIE Fighter: Defender of the Empire— Official Secrets & Solutions	$12.95
Thunderscape: The Official Strategy Guide	$19.95
Ultima: The Avatar Adventures	$19.95
Ultima VII and Underworld: More Avatar Adventures	$19.95
Under a Killing Moon: The Official Strategy Guide	$19.95
WarCraft: Orcs & Humans Official Secrets & Solutions	$9.95
Warlords II Deluxe: The Official Strategy Guide	$19.95
Werewolf Vs. Commanche: The Official Strategy Guide	$19.95
Wing Commander I, II, and III: The Ultimate Strategy Guide	$19.95
X-COM Terror From The Deep: The Official Strategy Guide	$19.95
X-COM UFO Defense: The Official Strategy Guide	$19.95
X-Wing: Collector's CD-ROM— The Official Strategy Guide	$19.95

TO ORDER BOOKS

Please send me the following items:

Quantity	Title	Unit Price	Total
_____	_____	$_____	$_____
_____	_____	$_____	$_____
_____	_____	$_____	$_____
_____	_____	$_____	$_____
_____	_____	$_____	$_____
_____	_____	$_____	$_____

	Total
Subtotal	$_____
7.25% Sales Tax (CA only)	$_____
8.25% Sales Tax (TN only)	$_____
5.0% Sales Tax (MD only)	$_____
7.0% G.S.T. Canadian Orders	$_____
Shipping and Handling*	$_____
TOTAL ORDER	$_____

*$4.00 shipping and handling charge for the first book, and $1.00 for each additional book.

By telephone: With Visa or MC, call 1-916-632-4400. Mon.–Fri. 9–4 PST. **By mail:** Just fill out the information below and send with your remittance to:

PRIMA PUBLISHING
P.O. Box 1260BK
Rocklin, CA 95677-1260

Satisfaction unconditionally guaranteed

Name_____

Address_____

City_____ State_____ Zip_____

Visa /MC#_____Exp._____

Signature_____

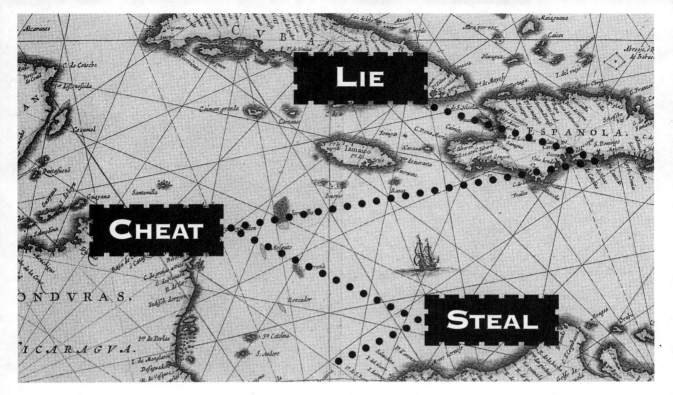

LIE

CHEAT

STEAL

Experience nation building at its best.

Enticed by the lure of exploring the unknown, you cross treacherous seas in search of the New World. But be warned! Europe's other conquering heroes are in pursuit of the same glory.

Conquest of the New World™ is a single or multi-player strategy game where you're in command of the explorers, settlers, and mercenary soldiers destined to survey the land, to build new colonies, and to protect your emerging nation. As you search for new rivers and mountains, you'll come across other colonies and encounter friendly and hostile native tribes. Your growing nation is constantly at the mercy of world events and the endless threat of surprise attacks.

Becoming a New World power takes cunning, ambition and the courage to venture into uncharted lands. Go too far, attack the wrong colony, or break a treaty and you could be faced with other colonial powers banding together to destroy you. Only through a perfect balance of diplomacy, exploration, trade and warfare can you build the ultimate nation, declare independence, and experience the true power of Conquest.

QUICKSILVER®
SOFTWARE, INC.

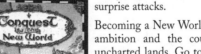

BY GAMERS. FOR GAMERS.™

Interplay Productions
17922 Fitch Ave.
Irvine, CA 92714
714-553-6678
Manufactured in the U.S.A.

CONQUEST OF THE NEW WORLD™
DOWNLOAD THE INTERACTIVE DEMO AT WWW.INTERPLAY.COM